TRAINING THE
GILBERT AND SULLIVAN CHORUS

TRAINING THE
GILBERT AND SULLIVAN
CHORUS

by

WILLIAM COX-IFE

Price, $2.00

CHAPPELL
& CO · INC·
RKO BUILDING
ROCKEFELLER
CENTER·N·Y·C
CHAPPELL
MADE IN U S A   &CO·LTD·LONDON

*To the Chorus of the D'Oyly Carte
Opera Company 1952-1955, who have
already heard it all.*

Printed in Great Britain by
Lowe & Brydone (Printers) Limited, London, N.W.10

William Cox-Ife was trained at the Royal Academy of Music where he studied conducting with Sir Henry J. Wood. His other subjects were piano and singing.

Until the outbreak of war he conducted many musical societies in London and was an accompanist and vocal coach. He broadcast regularly from the early days of the BBC, and his work in the theatre included a season for the Bristol Old Vic.

He served overseas in the Intelligence Corps, and since 1946 conducted regularly and arranged the scores for light operas and revues on the BBC television service. He has also been music director for many films.

He has conducted symyhony concerts in Germany with both the Bonn and the Rhineland Symphony Orchestras. He has also conducted for the Belgian Radio Service.

He joined the D'Oyly Carte Opera Company in 1951 as chorus master and assistant music director.

TO THE READER

England's musical genius produced the first ballad operas, a delight that, although neglected today, is not wholly forgotten. Much later, but surely as a logical progression appeared the comic operas of Gilbert and Sullivan, the finest light operas in the world and a proud part of our national heritage.

Out of my experience here is a book for the many chorus masters who train G. and S. choruses every year throughout the English speaking world. The precepts I give in Part I (Technical) can be applied to any chorus in any opera, light or grand, but the examples given are all from the G. and S. operas. In Part 2, I have given a working analysis of each of the operas most usually performed, and you will need the vocal scores by you for reference.

One more point. For " chorus master " you can always read " musical director ".

WILLIAM COX-IFE
CHELSEA, 1952-3.

FOREWORD

Mr. Cox-Ife has certainly written a book that one feels sure will be of interest and help to the many Musical Directors and Chorus Masters who tackle amateur productions of the Gilbert and Sullivan Operas in this Country, throughout the Commonwealth and also in America.

In these Operas it is the chorus that generally tells the story and creates the atmosphere in which the principals play; many members of the chorus are, in fact, separate characters, all of whom have special significance, both musically and dramatically; it is therefore essentially the sparkle, precision and audibility of the chorus that is of fundamental importance in creating the response in the audience that is necessary for the development of the principal characters.

I feel that Mr. Cox-Ife has much to say that should be helpful in obtaining sincere and intelligent singing and a sound balance between the demands of the libretti and of the music, not only for the works of Gilbert and Sullivan, but also for other types of musical production. It is, of course, upon this unity that the success of any such production depends.

BRIDGET D'OYLY CARTE

CONTENTS

INTRODUCTION

A first-class chorus is of vital importance in the performance of light opera. Especially is this true in those greatest examples of all, the Gilbert and Sullivan operas, affectionately known throughout the English speaking world as G. and S.

Function

A cursory glance at Gilbert's libretti shows that the chorus has two functions to fulfil; that of setting the scene, and that of supporting the principals in the action.

If the chorus fails completely to fulfil these two functions, not only will there be gaps in the story which leave the audience bewildered, but also any principal on his entrance will face an ill-informed and therefore unresponsive audience. No principal should have to tolerate such conditions, as his whole attention must be concentrated on his own share of the performance.

Qualifications

What then are the qualifications of a first class chorus?

1. Intelligence. For given intelligence, good directors (music and stage) can make good performers.

2. Voices. I place this qualification second advisedly, for I have encountered in my many years in theatre, film, radio and television, many fine voices without a vestige of intelligence to support them. If a chorus is a large one, such as in grand opera, where music is of primary importance, they can be of use; but in G. and S. light operas where music and stage hold equal rights, such members are a definite drawback. Their lack of imagination and sensibility is always very obvious to an audience.

3. Appearance. Satisfactory appearance does not imply a chorus of glamour girls and matinee idols, but a chorus of young people with personality and animation. Such people will also have enthusiasm and it is from this material, first class performer-singers are made.

4. Technical Qualifications. It is essential that the chorus members have a sound vocal technique. If not, it is difficult, perhaps impossible, to obtain subtleties of interpretation and phrasing, and ill-trained choristers are liable to damage their vocal chords. Stage movement and dancing can be taught in class, but not vocal technique.

It will also mean less drudgery for the chorus master if they can sight read.

Performance

In light opera there must be in both music and dialogue, attack, variety of speed and vocal colour and, above all, gaiety. For then the stage will sparkle.

There are also in G. and S. moments of drama where the atmosphere of the playing must equal that of the finest straight acting.

Not only the voice of each singer but the face and the stance of the whole body must be a complete expression or reflection of the moment. Also, even in repose, the eyes must remain alive, thereby showing a mental reaction to the scene.

Training

By tackling the three most important aspects of ensemble singing in the following order, truly brilliant performance will be achieved.

(a) Beautiful Vocal Sound. This, of course, is the foundation upon which to build, and beauty is the yardstick by which this basis is assessed. Volume without beauty is just noise.

(b) Impeccable Rhythm and Diction. I mention these two together as they are the interdependent. (see Later chapter.)

(c) The " thought behind ". Or as it is more usually called " interpretation ".

I don't care for this last word as it so often implies a superimposition of vocal tricks, so called " expression ", on to the vocal line. This is wrong. True interpretation is never adopted from without, but comes from within, being the result of imaginative thought.

Every word sung, every gesture, every stance must have a reason in order that it shall " come into being ". And the key which opens the door of reason is " thought ". Unless performers are drilled incessantly in " the reason ", the performance, no matter how brilliant it may be technically, will be insincere, and although it may dazzle it will fail to move and convince an audience. I maintain that without an impassioned sincerity, no work can be worth while, nor can it truly reach the heart of an audience.

This fact is not easy to instil into the players of light opera, which is chiefly comedy and satire, but the intelligent person will be convinced by a close study of the performance of a great comedian, such as Charles Chaplin. The rest is up to the directors.

Direction

In all theatre work there must be complete fusion of views between the music and stage directors. If their intentions are not agreed, performers cannot give of their best, for no man can serve two masters.

Any divergence of opinion must be resolved completely and finally, in private conference before rehearsals begin. Even small differences of opinion appearing during rehearsals, are better left to be discussed later in private. Neither director should impinge upon the other's domain in giving direction to the chorus or principals. The directors themselves must always see each other's point of view and each must be prepared to give way if at any difficult place, music must be subordinated to drama or vice versa.

In G. and S. such problems are few and far between as the authors worked together from the first conception of the story. Any doubt as to how a musical scene should be played will easily be dispelled by a study of the words and music as a whole, and not independently. I am fully aware that in most matters artistic more than one solution can be offered to a problem, but in G. and S. there is usually only one—the right one.

As an example I recall Phoebe's song in the " Yeomen of the Guard " " Were I thy bride ". Should this song, the climax of a scene of delightful light comedy, be treated as a broad comedy number and be played for laughs? What have Gilbert and Sullivan given us in this song?

Gilbert, a lyric of teasing tender beauty, of delicate analogies. From Sullivan we get possibly one of his most inspired settings. A lovely lilting melody, with an accompaniment that has the mark of genius, scored with subtlety of the highest order: a setting that was the result of much experiment and thought. Is this all to be lost in the laughter of an audience at commonplace antics? Or are we to savour to the full the charm of the lyric and the beauty of the music as well as delicately played comedy? I myself prefer to hear Gilbert and Sullivan.

Phoebe's Song: " The skylark's trill
Stanzas 6 *and* 7   Were but discordance shrill
V.S. Page 70   To the soft thrill
                             Of wooing as I'd woo—
                             Were I thy bride!

                             The roses sigh
                             Were as a carrion's cry
                             To lullaby
                             Such as I'd sing to thee,
                             Were I thy bride!"

REHEARSING

The Chorus Master

1.   The Chorus Master must, for his part, know his score thoroughly. Any problems encountered by the members must be resolved at once. There must be no hesitation on the part of the chorus master in presenting the resolution, and this can only be ensured if he has analysed the score thoroughly, from both artistic and technical angles, before the first rehearsal.

2.   He must be the possessor of good baton technique, and he must instruct the chorus in the interpretation of the movements of his baton, and train them to follow his conducting by the eye.

No body of singers can sing with attack, rhythm and polish on the stage, unless these virtues are to be found in the conductor's beat. The chorus must be responsive to the beat, so that their performance is flexible and alive, and never mechanical.

They must be trained " when " and " how " to look at the beat without destroying the stage illusion, and what to do in cases of musical mishap.

3.   Another essential quality in a first-class chorus master is the ability to excite the interest of his choristers, and, by his own attitude to the work in hand, whip them to a state of enthusiasm.

4.   A reason must always be offered for any instruction given. For if the reason is not clear in a performer's mind the performance cannot be sincere.

5.   Patience is another essential quality for success. Do not fail to realise that individuals differ from one another, and make allowances for this difference. Don't be too aloof to offer, within reason, individual help.

Be encouraging. For then should the occasion arise to criticise sternly, and this happens with even the best choruses, the effect will be salutary. A quiet, pleasant, authoritative manner, will achieve more than shouting.

6.   He should also have a practical knowledge of stagecraft and a sense of drama. These two attributes will enable him to co-operate sympathetically with the stage director.

Finally: The chorus master must show by his whole approach to his work an impassioned sincerity and belief in the work being prepared, and a never-failing striving for perfection. In this lies the secret of artistic achievement.

Rehearsals

At all rehearsals there must be firm discipline. Unpunctuality must never be allowed, nor must choristers be permitted to chat among themselves.

Always allow your chorus a break of ten to fifteen minutes in the middle of a session. This allows them to relax and pays dividends.

When necessary, rehearse your chorus in sections and do not be afraid to rehearse even two or three members at a time if you think they are not pulling their weight.

Blend of voices is an attribute of a good chorus, and this must not be neglected in a theatre chorus. Teach your members to blend their voices first as a section. Do not allow any individual voice to stand out above the rest. Then get sopranos and altos to sing together with blend and balance. Similarly, tenors and basses, and then the whole chorus.

SECTION ONE
TECHNICAL

ENSEMBLE SINGING FOR THE THEATRE

The following are the numbers required to constitute a first-class theatre chorus:

Sopranos	10	Divided as follows:		6	first
				4	second
Altos	8	,,	,, ,,	3	first
				5	second
Tenors	8	,,	,, ,,	5	first
				3	second
Basses	10	,,	,, ,,	4	first
				6	second

N.B. Make certain that all your second voices have a good middle and lower register. Don't overload your sopranos and tenors with voices that are all " top " or your chorus singing will lack richness of texture.

Beautiful Vocal Tone and Nuance

It is not necessary, I feel sure, to offer details of such training, as these can be found in any standard book on choir training. Better still, a well qualified chorus master will be the possessor of considerable vocal technique, and thus can draw on his own knowledge.

A point to be emphasised again and again is, that beauty of tone is the gauge of all singing, and care must be taken that even the loudest of fortissimi is still beautiful. In addition, this will prevent any forcing of tone, which damages the vocal chords.

Watch your choristers' breathing. This is essential, as one allows them to rehearse sitting down. Don't let them slump. They must sit upright. Don't hesitate, if it is felt necessary, to start a rehearsal with one or two simple breathing exercises.

Rhythm and Diction

(1) RHYTHM

Because in vocal music words are sung rhythmically instead of spoken freely, rhythm must receive especial care whilst notes and words are being taught. The finer points of performance come later. Great attention, however, must be paid to note values and intonation right from the start; for it is easier to get a correct note *in*, than an incorrect note *out* of a person's mind.

A performance which is lacking in rhythm is either dull and lifeless, or distorted.

Rhythm is the ever-moving stream which carries the notes to their fulfilment. Sometimes the stream may be a gentle brook, at other times, a rushing torrent. There may even be moments when all movement appears to stop in a placid pool, sooner or later to move on again,

In vocal music this pulsation is inseparable from the words. For, as a musical phrase must be correctly turned, so must a verbal phrase.

1

In G. and S. the musical setting of the words is of such a high standard that rarely does one have to compromise on either musical or " verbal " grounds. The syllabic stress required for an intelligent statement of a verbal passage invariably falls on the corresponding musical accent.

e.g.   Rec. Inez—Act 2 " Gondoliers " (V.S. page 214)—" The Royal Prince ";
Duet Phyllis and Strephon—Act 2 " Iolanthe " (V.S. page 160)—" If we're weak enough to tarry ".

The above are two examples of the care with which Sullivan set Gilbert's libretti. The recitative can be sung with the most meticulous attention to note values and still sound quite conversational. It is set exactly as an actor would speak the lines dramatically.

The duet fairly dances along, and the lyric can be given its full due, whilst the singers remain faithful to the music. Another delightful example is the song I quoted earlier; Phoebe's " Were I thy bride " in Act I of " Yeomen of the Guard ".

Great artists are always able to give great performances within the musical framework. They know that to step out of the framework distorts the rhythm, and without perfect rhythm there can be no style, no elegance, and these operas must have both.

(2) DICTION

These early rehearsals over, the chorus should now be drilled in diction. This is not a matter that can be taught in a few rehearsals, but one that has to be a long term policy, calling for constant watchfulness on the part of the chorus master and the chorister. The choristers too, must practise on their own to acquire the requisite flexibility of tongue and lips that is necessary if the words are to be clear.

There are two basic faults which are accountable for most of the incoherent singing heard today in the theatre, as well as the concert hall, not forgetting radio! One, bad vowel sounds, and two, a complete failure to enunciate final consonants.

(i) Correcting Bad Vowel Sounds

Bad vowel sounds cannot be fully corrected at chorus rehearsals. A great improvement, however, can be made if the chorus master demonstrates the correct shape of mouth and position of tongue for each vowel, but he must take the chief offenders on their own, give them a few simple exercises, and insist upon daily practice. Such exercises can be found in any standard book on speech.

(ii) Final Consonants

Take for example the opening of the " Gondoliers " . . . " List and learn " . . . " Roses white and roses red ". How often is heard " Lisanlear " . . . " Roses whian roses re ". This is usually the result of bad or ill-digested teaching of singing; the pupil's attention being focussed upon vowel sounds and forgetting, if ever told, that consonants must also be sung. Of course, the explosive consonants such as " D " and " T " cannot be sung in the strict sense, but the labials not only can, but must be sung, if a good vocal line as well as clear diction is to be achieved.

To return to the " Gondoliers " opening chorus for the girls : " List and learn ". In these three words we have problems of diction which, if solved, will give the key to the solution of many difficult passages.

The first difficulty is the " N " of " learn ". It will be found that although the singers are trying, the " N " is still not heard. The reason is that they are ceasing to sing too early. In order to sound an " N " the tip of tongue has to be brought to the palate immediately behind the front teeth, and it is not completed until the tongue has dropped down once more. Singers have a bad habit of ceasing to sing while the tongue is still in the upper position. This will never produce a clear consonant. The singing must stop a split second after the tongue has dropped. If the voice continues too long we will get " N—er ". Practice, however, will give the correct timing, and the audience will hear the " N " with no " —er " following it.

Inexperienced singers will imagine that when they are pronouncing a final consonant correctly, they are exaggerating; the chorus master must convince them that only a skilled listener, and not the performer, is in the position to judge. A good rule to give the performer is: slight exaggeration sounds normal to the audience: merely " correct " final consonants will not carry beyond the singer's ears! They must take the chorus master's word in this matter and not trust their own judgment, for what the performer himself hears is totally different from what the audience hears in the back row of the circle.

In this test phrase we have further problems: the "—nd " of " and ". This is solved in exactly the same way as the " n " in " learn ", but there is the added difficulty of the final consonant of one word being followed in quick succession by the initial consonant of the next: the " l " of " learn ". With our nationally slack way of speaking, the " d " of "—nd " is automatically dropped. The chorus must be made to practise, slowly at first, the two words, so that we hear " nd "—" l ", with the tongue dropping after " and ", and being raised again for the " l " of " learn ". Make sure in this " slow motion " singing, the vocal tone continues between the words.

Finally, the matter of the " t " in " list ". The early attempts to sound the " t " will result in " lis-tand ". This must not be allowed. It is caused by the " and" being sung as the tongue descends. Only by waiting until the tongue is fully descended before singing " and " can the words be separated.

This problem of separating a clearly sounded final consonant from the initial vowel sound of the following word, is a constant worry, and must never be passed over.

Sometimes, through excess of enthusiasm, choristers when singing words which end in " r " will roll this consonant. Stop this at once. Final " r's " are always mute.

PRECEPT.—A warning to chorus masters. Be sure you can accurately demonstrate these points before you rehearse your chorus. If you can't they will quite naturally presume you are asking the impossible. In other words—that you don't know what you are talking about.

Initial Consonants

Further, if a clean attack and ensemble is to be achieved, there must be no lingering on initial consonants. The singer must open immediately onto the vowel sound, e.g., Act 2 " Yeomen of the Guard " (V.S. page 112)

" Night has spread her pall once more ".

If there is not an instantaneous opening onto the " i ", the result is " nnnn-night ". In Act 1, the funeral scene, the final " Oh mercy " (V.S. page 98) must be sung in the same way. This is a very dangerous spot as the word " mercy " is spread over five slow beats. The singers must open straight onto the " er " and the " cy ", exactly on the first beat of each bar.

The Meaning of the Words

To clarity of pronunciation must now be added intelligence of delivery, and in singing we must give the same syllabic stress to a sentence, as would be given were that sentence spoken.

Consider the opening bars of " The Pirates of Penzance ". This is set to a typical Sullivan quick 6/8 melody, and, if sung badly, sounds dull and lumpy. A quick 6/8 is an essentially springy rhythm, and if the syllables which fall on the strong beats are merely mechanically emphasised with no thought for the verbal sense, the result, despite clear enunciation of words, is unintelligible. If, however, the meaning of the words is borne in mind and the first two lines are given as a definite request, intelligent verbal phrasing and stylish musical phrasing will result.

This accenting of essential syllables will give the stanza life and meaning. The crescendo indications, must be regarded as crescendos of intensity, rather than volume. (See Appendix A.)

It is only by this method of placing accents that the meaning of each phrase becomes clear. Remember a bar line does not necessarily precede a heavily marked beat. The " strong " beats (this term is used in its academic meaning) must be regarded as a series of springboards from which the music progresses from bar to bar. The falling of a note (or word) on a strong beat must have the same result as an acrobat or diver, jumping on a springboard. The moment of impact is the beginning of an upward and forward movement. Thus does music progress from beat to beat, always moving, sometimes fast and sometimes slow, but never, except on a pause, remaining still.

Any other conception of the function of beats, or any marking of accents by a downward emphasis, is wrong, and will result in unmusical and unrhythmic performance.

When singing a slow passage even greater care has to be taken to avoid a four-square effect. For example in the Finale Act 1 of " Patience " (page 87 V.S.) Lady Angela, on seeing Grosvenor for the first time, sings:

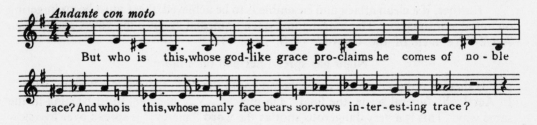

The first half of this phrase is repeated by the chorus. Unless the chorus has been well trained, the verbal stress will be like this:

"Yes who is this, whose God-like grace proclaims he comes of noble race."

It is a pity that Sullivan did not mark the phrasing that he so obviously intended.

It is, however, quite simple to phrase intelligently and musically if the meaning of the words is borne in mind:

Legato

"Yes who is this, whose God like grace proclaims he comes of noble race."

The verbal stress is exactly as it would sound were the words spoken in a manner of wonderment. This would avoid any suggestion of, say, "of noble race," which is just thoughtless and stupid.

If this turning point of the drama, the sudden adoration by the " love-sick maidens " for this " apostle of simplicity " is to be convincing, this passage must be sung tenderly and with a beautiful mezza voce.

Sullivan uses 6/8 and 2/4 rhythms very frequently in all his comic operas, and example, in the finale Act 1 " Pirates of Penzance " (V.S. page 81) there is the added difficulty of considerable stage movement. In spite of stage action, however, this music can be delivered by principals and chorus in such a manner that neither words nor meaning are lost to the audience. The 6/8 section must be sung cleanly and with a lilt.

After Ruth's scene and exit, the end section written in ₵ will well repay care and attention, for the words must be heard:

> " Here's a *first* rate oppor*tun*ity
> To get *mar*ried with im*pun*ity
> And in*dul*ge in the fe*lic*ity
> Of Un*boun*ded domes*tic*ity
> We will *quic*kly be par*son*ified
> *Con*jugally *mat*rimo*nified
> By a *Doc*tor of *Divin*ity
> Who re*sides* in this *vicin*ity ".

It will be seen that the accents as marked, coincide in every line, except the fourth and eighth which have additional accents, with the normal accentuation expected in duple time. The guide as to where accents are to be placed must be the meaning of the verbal phrase.

If this precept is disregarded the sense of the phrase may be obscured and, in extreme cases, altered, as many an author has found to his dismay.

THE THOUGHT BEHIND THE WORDS

Precept—It is not so much what you say, but what you think when you say it, that gives life to your performance.

Only by intense thought and thorough rehearsing can a performer step out of his own personality into that of the character he is portraying. This creative effort, and it is an effort, both on the part of the performers and directors, is as necessary for the humblest member of the chorus as for the star. But in this lies the secret of real performance.

In G. and S. operas the chorus is never used as padding or mere spectacular effect. Their every appearance on the stage is an integral part of the story and their presence and performance (vocal and physical) is absolutely vital in building towards the climax of the finales. They must be convinced of their own importance in the operas, and whilst working as a team, still exist as individuals. Choristers must, therefore, be convinced that there is a reason for every word, sung or spoken, and every gesture made.

At this stage of rehearsals, the members of the chorus should be given a general picture of the opera in preparation, and their function as a body, explained to them. It is the responsibility of the chorus master to do this.

Consider the opera " Patience ". The opening chorus sung by " twenty love sick maidens ", with solos by Angela and Ella, sets the whole atmosphere of this aesthetic satire. The singing, costumes and attitudes all contribute towards the story, and if the audience is to have a clear picture before them from the rise of the curtain, the chorus must make certain that their every word and gesture is clean-cut. The dialogue between Lady Jane, Angela and Patience, merely continues the plot.

This scene is followed by the entrance of the Dragoons, a complete contrast to the world of aesthetic art in which the ladies are living. With the Dragoons, swagger is the order of the day, and it is they who provide, in every way, the antidote to the artificiality of Bunthorne and Grosvenor and the deliberately exaggerated stupidity of the ladies.

The next scene, the entrance of Bunthorne and the maidens, with the Dragoons looking on in bewilderment at the incredible spectacle of their ex-fiancees' infatuation with the long-haired poet, is one which further develops the theme of the story, and it is a scene which requires strong contrast between the aesthetic and the earthy.

After the Colonel's song, which closes this section of the opera, the chorus does not appear until the finale of Act 1. In this finale they are at all times concerned with the action as individuals and not as spectators, for each Dragoon has his ex-fiancee among the girls. Only Bunthorne and Patience speak for themselves. Whenever the Colonel or the Duke speaks, it is on behalf of all the Dragoons: and so with Lady Jane and Angela—they speak not only for themselves but for all the ladies. Consequently, as all are concerned, all have a reason for acting to the utmost of their capacity.

In Act 2, with the exception of Grosvenor's song and the very short finale, the play is only concerned with the leading characters, so the remainder of the company do not appear.

Having given the chorus a general picture such as this, the chorus master has now reached the stage of rehearsing when he must teach its members to think correctly.

This does not mean thinking of technique: that should be done at earlier rehearsals and while practising alone and must be put on one side at later rehearsals and at performances. Technique must be so sound that it becomes a conditioned reflex once the curtain rises. The thought required at performance is that which gives the reason underlying every statement, sung or spoken, every gesture, and every entrance or exit made. For it is only when the thought is correct that a sincere, convincing performance is given. Never must a performer approach any scene, or attempt to sing any phrase, with the idea in his mind " What do I do to get this over ": " What vocal trick will give my voice the right colour: express the correct emotion "? Such an approach results in insincerity, and is therefore unconvincing.

As an example of how to instil correct thinking into a chorus take " The Peers' Chorus " from " Iolanthe " (V.S. page 36)

Here is a number in which can be found all the elements which go to make an exciting piece of stage presentation. Words, music, costume and decor, are of the finest theatrical quality. It is regrettable to have to add that even an uninspired performance will not completely destroy the scene. It is a great compliment to the material when even a poor presentation can get by. If, however, the performance is all that it should be, there is an electric atmosphere in the theatre, for which both stage and audience are equally responsible.

In this example, the excitement of anticipation starts with the roll of the side drums. Then the opening chords are heard and up-stage begins the procession of the Peers. From this moment the men of the chorus dressed in Peers' robes must behave like Gilbert's Peers. Their bearing, walk, and haughty expression must be in keeping with the sentiments they will shortly express in their singing.

They must, in order to exude that air of aristocratic superiority, try, not only during the time they are on the stage, but also while waiting for their entrance, to look upon life through the eyes of one whose spiritual home was that stronghold of Victorian predjudice, the House of Lords. They should stand and walk in a dignified manner, not because the director has told them to, but because they, superior creatures, hold themselves aloof from the public, and in no circumstances would they unbend or relax. Theirs is the " airy condescension " of Lord Tolloller, together with the " self-contained dignity " of Lord Mountararat. They introduce themselves with the simple conceit of expressing repeatedly the basic tenets of their creed:

> " Loudly let the trumpet bray
> 　　Tantantara
> Proudly bang the sounding brasses
> 　　Tzing boom
> As upon its lordly way
> This unique procession passes
> 　　Tantantara Tzing boom.
>
> We are the peers of highest station
> Paragons of legislation
> Pillars of the British nation
> 　　Tantantara Tzing boom."

The use of " thought " as the motive power of all performance, apart from showing the correct way to characterisation, also helps the performer to avoid certain dangerous pitfalls.

Often one sees a performer of considerable technical equipment who spends the whole of his time listening to himself. Usually this person has a beautiful voice and excellent technique. Probably, at the beginning of his career, he listened to himself in order to check his delivery, but finally he became so " self " conscious that he excluded any other approach to performance. This type is monotonous in the extreme.

Another pitfall, the danger of staleness at either prolonged rehearsals or a long run in the theatre, will be avoided automatically, if the thought is kept alive in the performer. No one who thinks correctly, that is to say one who is truly in character, can either " walk through " a performance, or be bored. The atmosphere of a play or opera is kept alive, only when the minds of all the performers are alert. Furthermore, a dull audience can be shaken out of their dullness, if the performers project their performance with this mental impetus.

Is there such a thing as a bad audience, or is this the natural outcome of a bad performance?

THE PATTER REFRAIN

In many of the G. and S. operas the chorus is called upon to sing refrains, sometimes short and sometimes long, written in the style of the patter song. In the musical setting of such refrains it is found that, with few exceptions, every syllable of every word is sung to a note of equal value—a quaver or semi-quaver. And the tempo is always fast.

It is difficult for a chorus to sing these refrains rhythmically, with clear diction and intelligent verbal point. Given flexible voices and clear enunciation, training on the following lines will produce the result required for a good performance.

Having taught your choristers to sing the correct notes and words at a reduced tempo, the first step towards singing quickly is to avoid over-vocalisation. This does not necessarily mean singing softly but singing with the minimum vocal effort required to make each note heard at whatever degree of loudness is indicated. This reduction of vocalisation by reducing the pressure of breath must be compensated by a corresponding increase in verbal projection.

This golden rule must never be broken.

Now that the chorus can sing a patter refrain quickly, it will be found that instead of maintaining a steady tempo, they tend to get quicker and quicker. This is partially due to the difficulty of snatching a breath at the end of a verbal phrase when no allowance, such as a rest, has been made in the music. Therefore, insist that the choristers stagger their breathing. That is, they avoid taking a breath all at the same time.

Before I give the complete solution to our problem, consider for the moment what exactly Gilbert and Sullivan have written in this typical example from " Iolanthe "—Finale Act 1 (V.S. page 98).

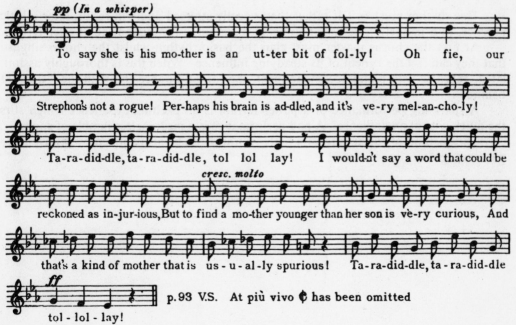

To say she is his mo-ther is an ut-ter bit of fol-ly! Oh fie, our

Strephon's not a rogue! Per-haps his brain is ad-dled, and it's ve-ry mel-an-cho-ly!

Ta-ra-did-dle, ta-ra-did-dle, tol lol lay! I would-n't say a word that could be

reckoned as in-jur-ious, But to find a mo-ther younger than her son is ve-ry curious, And

that's a kind of mother that is us-u-al-ly spurious! Ta-ra-did-dle, ta-ra-did-dle

tol - lol - lay!

p. 93 V.S. At più vivo ¢ has been omitted

9

Here we have a long succession of quavers in alla breve time which, according to our musical text-books, gives us a strong beat at the beginning of every bar. But in patter refrains, as in all vocal music, to give automatic stress at the beginning of every bar, irrespective of verbal stress, is wrong. Moreover, even if this stress is made it will not entirely help the choristers to keep a steady tempo. By studying the words, it will be seen that there is a broader rhythmic framework upon which these quavers are hung. I call this the " Basic Rhythm ".

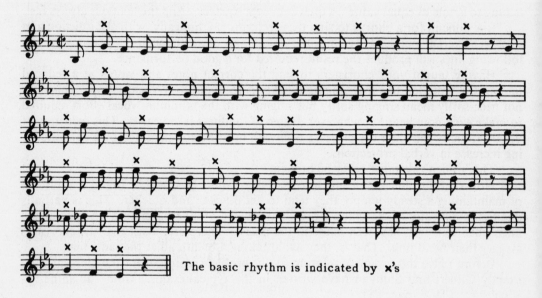

The basic rhythm is indicated by **x**'s

This rhythm must be felt rather than vocally stressed and will result, after a little practice, in a perfectly steady tempo being maintained throughout any patter refrain.

At first the chorus master must clap the basic rhythm whilst the chorus sing, so that they can feel the benefit of its steadying influence. When this is thoroughly assimilated, rehearse with piano accompaniment, the correct nuance and with the " thought behind ".

A sparkling performance of a patter refrain is an exciting experience which stirs the quick wits of an audience. A bad performance is a meaningless jumble of sound.

This method of learning to sing patter refrains can be also applied by principals to patter songs.

MUSIC AND MOVEMENT

By " music " I mean the sung word: by " movement " I mean gesture and what the stage director calls " business ".

Movement on the stage, to be convincing, must have meaning and reason, both of which are to be found in the words, spoken or sung. Movement should be a logical development of the music.

In no circumstance is it permissible to regard music and movement as separate aspects of a work, which must be superimposed one upon the other. Such an attitude on the part of the directors (music and stage) not only will lead to intolerable arguments, but will result in a marionette-like performance at the best, or a ragged performance at the worst, both divorced from " meaning and reason ".

Performers must see their work as a complete entity, and not as a combination of two different mediums of expression.

I now take it for granted that at this stage of rehearsing, the chorus has also been trained by the stage director or his assistant in the mechanics of simple movement, such training having been given, of course, without reference to any specific opera. They have been trained to stand correctly, walk with grace and reason, and make basic gestures dramatically.

In order that the business calls should be a logical continuation of the music calls, the music and stage directors must have resolved any differences of opinion in consultation, before any calls are made. They must be of one mind as to the presentation as a whole. It is, therefore, of the utmost importance to the stage director that the music director or chorus master, has an understanding of the theatrical situation, and that he gives in the music an accurate presentation of the drama. As I have said before this will avoid any possibility that the performers may feel they have to serve two masters—a fatal mood for any performance.

Now comes the moment in rehearsal when the chorus will be instructed in movements required in the numbers, and the stage director will give these in two parts.

First, a reference to the meaning or implication of the words. Second, how this is to be shown in movement as the words are sung.

Movement can be divided into three categories:—

(1) Movements which help depict a character, e.g., the opening chorus of the " Mikado ": the " Gentlemen of Japan " with their puppet-like gestures; or the aesthetic poses of the maidens in " Patience ".

(2) Movements that are dramatic, e.g. Katisha's entrance in Act 1 of the " Mikado " and the reaction of the assembly; or the finale of Act 1 " Gondoliers " to the chorus of " Then hail, oh King ".

(3) Movements which are an expression of mood, e.g., the dance steps which precede " The merriest fellows are we " in Act 1 of " Gondoliers ", which are an expression of gaiety: or the walk with folded arms and lowered heads in the funeral procession in " Yeomen of the Guard ", Act 1.

11

It is movements of the second category that directly rely upon the music, and only if the music is sung with the correct rhythmic attack and verbal emphasis, can the movements be the correct physical counterpart.

For example, in the Peers' chorus, on the words " Bow, bow, ye lower middle classes " (" Iolanthe " V.S. page 38), the Peers on the first " Bow " make a gesture with their right arms commanding obeisance. This gesture can only be made with the requisite authority, if the phrase is sung with equivalent meaning. The gesture must always be a reflection of the verbal attack.

A contrasting example is found in Act 2 of " H.M.S. Pinafore " when Ralph and Josephine are about to elope. The sailors enter on tip-toe singing " Carefully on tip-toe ". Only if this is sung in a truly conspiritorial manner will the walk be equally conspiritorial.

FOCUS OF ATTENTION

Focus of attention is the focal point towards which all reaction is directed at any given moment.

Although this subject is essentially the business of the stage director, I feel it is to the advantage of all that the music director should not only understand the principles governing this facet of stage performance, but should guide the choristers during music rehearsals in this matter.

It is only when correct focus of attention is held, that a satisfactory interplay of drama is achieved. With the exception of scenes in which one person is on the stage, all scenes consist of action and reaction between the actors, and in large scenes between the action of principals and the reaction of the crowd.

Reaction can be active or passive. The first is more obvious. e.g.—the gesture of terror on the entrance of Katisha, or the greeting of the two gondoliers by the crowd.

This obvious type of reaction naturally cannot be ignored or forgotten in any well-drilled company for it is essentially a physical reaction.

The second type, passive reaction, is not so obvious, for it implies no physical movement, but a focussing of thought upon the focal point of the scene.

E.g. In the Mikado's song the assembled company, with the exception of Katisha, all look towards the Mikado and listen. Only if this is done, is there reason for their repetition of the refrain. This example shows the importance of maintaining a focus of attention in an isolated scene, but even more important is the correct change of focus of attention in moving drama.

In the Finale of Act 2 in the " Gondoliers ", the whole company, except Luiz, enter while the Don introduces Inez, the nurse. From this moment the attention of all is focused upon her, as she slowly walks down stage and takes up her position. Then she sings the recitative " The Royal Prince ". The stage director probably visualizes this concentration of thought in the form of a diagram thus:

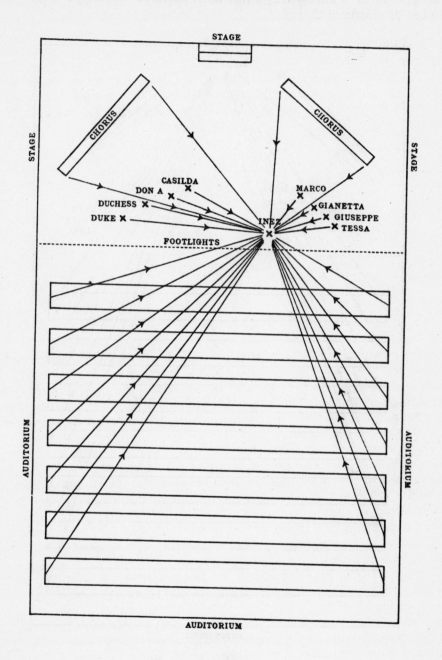

At the end of the recitative, Inez points to the dais up-stage and all, following her gesture, see Luiz standing there. Sullivan has marked the exact moment for this gesture and change of focus of attention by a fortissimo chord on the full orchestra. The new pattern can be visualized thus:

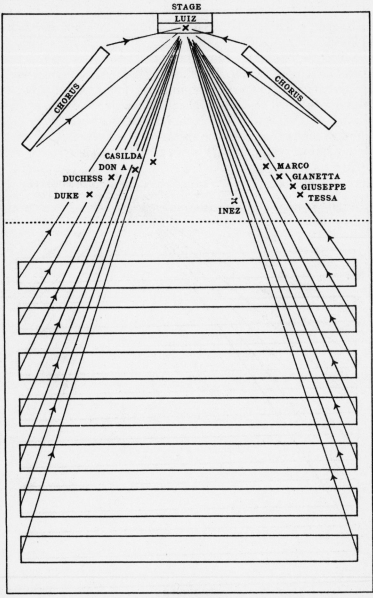

From this last example it is obvious how the kaleidoscopic effect of a sudden change of focus of attention made precisely at the correct moment in the music, heightens the drama. No less important is a gradual change of focus of attention; for as the performers' attention is held, so is that of the audience.

CODA

In the foregoing chapters I have given a scheme of training which will produce a first-class chorus.

As I said in the beginning, throughout this book for " chorus master " you can read " musical director " because the finest production is obtained when these two are in complete agreement on method of training and results to be desired. It is the musical director who has the final say at full rehearsals and his direction of the choral singing should be a logical continuation of the chorus master's work.

The musical director must direct at least one final rehearsal from the back of the circle while his assistant conducts. It is not possible to get a true perspective on a performance when standing in the orchestra pit, where balance between singing and orchestra, nuance, and diction, obviously cannot be judged correctly.

Know what you want and see that you get it, but don't forget to make the striving for perfection exciting.

SECTION TWO

WORKING ANALYSIS

"THE MIKADO"—ACT 1

No. 1 Opening Chorus

The justification of this brilliant opening chorus is to set the locality of the opera. There is no foreshadowing of the plot. It is, as can be heard in the opening words— "We are gentlemen of Japan" . . . the male chorus introducing themselves. The following lines:

> "If you think we are worked by strings,
> Like a Japanese marionette
> You don't understand these things
> It is simply court etiquette "

are not without a certain significance. For whilst admitting that their attitudes are formal to the point of being stilted, they are nevertheless "gentlemen of Japan". In other words . . . real persons and not mechanical dolls. Both performers and directors (music and stage) must remember these words and despite the automaton-like movements, there must be life and characterisation behind this "court etiquette".

It is of paramount importance that the performance of this chorus should be brilliant, not only for its own sake, but because a principal character, Nanki-Poo, enters as the chorus finishes, and the dramatic effect of his entry depends upon the contrast of this "very imperfect ablutioner" with the gentlemen of the court.

The singers must not only carry themselves as "gentlemen of Japan" but think of themselves as such. The walk to the positions taken on the stage, must be right if the singing is to be right. No one can walk like a peasant and sound like a lord. All the movements of the fans and the kneeling must be done with perfect precision, and the opening words:

"If you want to know who we are"

must be delivered with the crispness of a side-drum beat. Every singer must sound every consonant, with especial care on the " t's ". The brisk pace does not permit of the double " t " (" want to ") being sounded, but it is essential that one " t " is heard.

The utmost attention must be paid throughout to rhythm and length of notes. The singing must be non-legato, in order to give the vocal counterpart of the marionette-like figures, with their attitudes "queer and quaint".

Take note of the bars with the syncopated accents, and have the *sf's* clear. This can only be achieved without damage to the vocal chords by quick pressure from the diaphragm.

When the singing finishes, the chorus drop their automaton-like poses and walk

16

to the sides of the stage. This walk gives a sense of relaxation, but it must still be a dignified walk of gentlemen, who, on Nanki-Poo's entrance, suddenly freeze into haughty and enquiring poses. Should this walk be in any way slovenly, it breaks the continuity, so admirably expressed by the music, that Gilbert so obviously wanted, and it lessens the contrast between the " gentlemen " and the ragged " wandering Minstrel ".

It is not enough to have the sudden stillness on Nanki-Poo's first word " Gentlemen ", if the bearing demanded by the opening lyric has been allowed to droop. The moment of departure from " court etiquette " must be delayed until they join in Nanki-Poo's song. As far as they know Nanki-Poo is only a " very imperfect ablutioner " and, if anything, their attitude, both mental and physical, would be even more haughty and aloof than usual. The reply " Why who are you? " to Nanki-Poo's question should be delivered in a biting tone.

No. 2—" A Wandering Minstrel "

It is essential that Nanki-Poo is provided with this background of implacable disdain, in order that the charm of the minstrel himself will, by contrast, be more apparent. Furthermore, the justification for, and the effect of, his song becomes more marked as the reserve of the " gentlemen " is gradually broken down: first by gestures, " Are you in sentimental mood? ", second by repeating " We shouldn't be " and third in their rousing sea song chorus. After this chorus they, remembering their rank, become haughty once more.

The refrain " We shouldn't be surprised if nations trembled in alarm " must be sung with tremendous pride with a strongly marked crescendo on the 3rd and 4th bars. See Ex. 1.

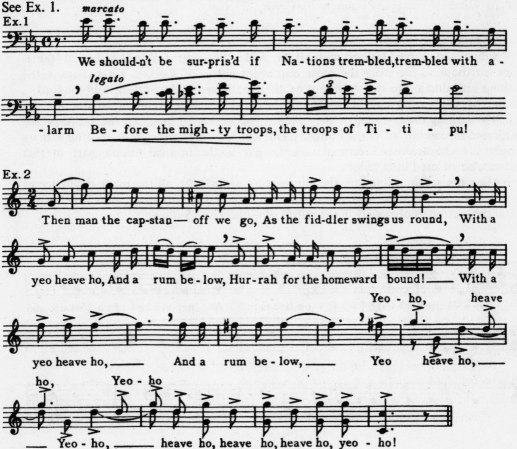

The chorus of the sea song (Ex. 2) must be very rhythmical throughout. The consonants on " Yeo-ho, heave ho " must be sung with enormous impetus. Only if this chorus is sung with vigour and impeccable rhythm, will the actions have the necessary controlled abandon, and be convincing. The final phrase of the song " With dreamy lullaby ", should be sung in a beautiful mezza voce.

No. 3 Song: Pish-Tush and Chorus

In this song the chorus do nothing except repeat the final bars of each verse. It is essential that there is no movement from them of any kind, during the song itself, for Pish-Tush is giving part of the plot and nothing must distract the audience from following it.

In this, as in all similar cases of the chorus repeating a line or two of a refrain, there must be no hint of a merely mechanical echo, but a live reiteration, which emphasizes the theme of the solo lines.

N.B. (1) Watch the semiquaver before the last note.
     (2) Do not allow ♪.'s to be cut short.

No. 5—Entrance of Ko-ko

Sullivan has served Gilbert with all the skill at his command in the musical framework for the first, therefore the most important entry, of Ko-ko. First there is the exciting introduction to the statement by the Gentlemen of Japan " Behold the lord ". At all costs the singing and the bearing of the chorus must be even more aristocratically haughty than at the opening of the opera. This serves to heighten the satire of the words and throws into relief the fluttering entry of Ko-ko, together with his song with its delightfully characterised accompaniment, that is the musical counterpart of this nervous, bewildered little tailor.

After his self-introduction, the chorus sing again, with all the mock-deference at their command. " Defer ", etc. Both music and stage directors must spare no effort to attain the picture so obviously in the minds of Gilbert and Sullivan.

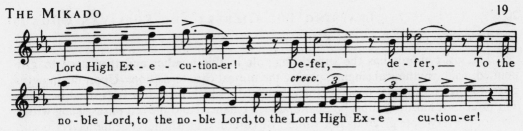

Lord High Ex - e - cu-tion-er! De-fer,___ de - fer,___ To the

no - ble Lord, to the no - ble Lord, to the Lord High Ex - e - cu-tion-er!

Ex.2 V.S. p.53 Ⓔ cresc. for 2 bars "Bow down, Bow down"

Ex.3

to the no - ble, no - ble Lord.___

No. 5A—"I've got a little list"

The repetitions of the final lines of each verse must be given clearly and rhythmically, in a rather patronising manner. There should be no unbending of the chorus gentlemen to Ko-ko at any time during the opera. They must hold aloof from " this cheap tailor ".

Let the accents fall on the first beat of every bar, until " they'll none of them be missed ", the last five words of each refrain to be given equal accents, in order to drive home the moral.

No. 6—Chorus of Girls

This chorus must be sung with the translucent innocence of young girls who are leaving the sheltered life of " little ladies ", and entering the outside world for the first time. They are round-eyed with wonder, a little afraid, but nevertheless bubbling over with excitement. The doubts they express must pass, as does a small cloud on a summer's day. The shadow, real as it is, is only transient. The singing must be gay and charming in the opening passages, " Comes a train of little ladies ", tender and questioning in " Is it but a world of trouble ". The singers must identify themselves completely with their stage characters, if their statements and questions are to be sincere.

Immaculate intonation, blend of voices, and phrasing are only the foundations of performance, but in themselves these are not enough. There must be thought behind the words and music, which will in effect turn stage puppets into real persons. Gay as the general effect of this number is, it is in fact quite poignant in its appeal for happiness.

The semiquaver passages should be rehearsed slowly, first sopranos, then contraltos, so that the notes are not slurred into each other but crystal clear, as if performed on two flutes. Make certain that all final consonants are sounded neatly. At letter (A) (V.S. page 61) " Is it but a world of trouble " should be sung molto legato with a carefully controlled crescendo and decrescendo, as marked. Similarly, " Is its beauty but a bubble ".

At (B) (V.S. page 61), do not allow the sopranos to breathe before " fantasies ": insist that they sing these four bars in one breath. Make sure you hear " fade " not " fay ". When the word " glory " is sung do not be satisfied until the true meaning of the word can be felt. A well-articulated " GL " will help considerably. There must be a touch of rapture in the singing of this word, which helps to mark the contrast of " Shadow of a shade ". Finally, " And we wonder " must be sung with happy, excited anticipation.

No. 7—Trio and Chorus

The girl's chorus has the supporting role in this number and they need to give pointed, neat, rhythmical singing, paying the utmost care to diction. Upon the impetus given to the consonants, depends the clarity with which these few bars must be sung. The three part harmony must be clear and well balanced and the last phrase sung with a rich tone, every note given its full value. Be careful that whenever semiquavers occur, they are not clipped:

No. 8—Quartet and Chorus

The above remarks apply equally to this number, with some additional points. In the " tra la la's " the rhythmic phrasing must be:

Tra la la la la la Tra *etc.*

In " But youth, of course, must have its fling ", ensure that the verbal commas after " youth " and " course " are observed, so that the excuse contained in this phrase is obvious. Sullivan's phrasing of the accompaniment, according to his own score, is not slurred. Therefore I feel he intended the phrase to be sung as I suggest. Strict observance of the commas, which does not mean clipping the notes short, or taking breaths in this phrase, helps to point the coquettishly teasing attitude of the girls towards Pooh-Bah.

The " Tra la la's " in harmony, must be accented thus:

FINALE—Act 1

This is probably the most dramatic finale to be found in the G. and S. operas. Both musical and stage directors must study it carefully so they have a clear picture in their minds of the dramatic shape in which it is cast. And in order that full justice be done to it, the singing and acting must be of the highest quality.

The opening " With aspect stern ", must be sung with the dark tone and ominous manner of impending fate. Special attention must be paid to the final consonants in the words " stride, decide, hesitate, name and same ". The chorus must tower above Ko-ko in voice and mien. A purposeful crescendo on "fate" when sung for the second time, is imperative, in order that this short episode be properly shaped.

The mood continues with Pooh-Bah's question " To ask you what you mean to do we punctually appear ", but is broken by Ko-ko's chirpy reply and the cheerful response of the chorus. The phrases " Hail, Nanki-Poo " and " Yes, yes, he'll do ", are sung with joyful relief.

After Ko-ko's next lines, with their transparently honest excuse sung in an ingratiating manner, the chorus agree with kindly mockery, " Ah yes he loves himself with passion tend'rer still." In order that the full effect of these lines be felt, they must be sung with a warm, rich tone, and with a crescendo on the first four notes of the first half of the phrase, and on the second half with a beautiful, telling, piano; absolute silence in the crotchet rest, and a very slight rit on " tend'rer still ".

The allegro con brio which follows must not be allowed to drag, The quintet must be sung with a joyous lilt, making certain that the balance is correct so that the melody line predominates. When the chorus enter the phrasing should be:

"With joyous shout

With joyous shout and ringing cheer

Inaugurate

Inaugurate their brief career "

In the remainder of the lines the sopranos must sing with increasing intensity the rising scale of minims, with the remainder of the chorus hammering out, with equal accents and with increasing intensity, the crotchets to the end of the phrase.

In the repeat of this section, mark as strongly as possible the syncopated bars at the end. It will help if the first crotchet of the second-time bar is cut short, and the singers snatch a quick breath. Do not let the sopranos slide over the quavers when they occur; these notes must be clearly and rhythmically sung.

After Pooh-Bah's solo the chorus once more crash in with their refrain, and this third repetition should be the most exciting all. At this point Katisha makes her dramatic entry and light hearted gaiety turns to drama of great intensity.

During the remainder of this finale are seen the efforts of Katisha to impose her will, not only upon Nanki-Poo, but upon all the assembled company. The mental struggles of the protagonists must be clearly drawn and the reactions of the company to Katisha's demands and threats, carefully built up to the climax of defiance in the last chorus " We do not heed their dismal sound."

The words and music are so beautifully written that even a bad performance cannot totally destroy their brilliance, but a performance worthy of the material has a breathtaking excitement which is probably unique in light opera repertoire.

As Katisha enters, the whole company cower with a shriek of terror, and with a rising note of fearful anger, sing, " Why, who is this whose evil eyes rain blight on our festivities? " It is not the volume of sound in this phrase which is so telling, but the feeling of almost uncontrollable terror behind the words. But before Katisha has finished her next phrase " I claim my perjured lover, Nanki-Poo ", the crowd are recovering their courage and they sing, more with anger than fear, " Go, leave thy deadly work undone." After Katisha's next phrase " Come back ", the company reply in commanding tones " Away, away, ill-favoured one ". This third phrase must be sung with greater tone than the preceding two; a break must be made after the first " Away " and the phrase spat out at Katisha.

Katisha then takes the stage with her song, " Oh fool that flee-est my hallowed joys ". She is the focus of attention, and her embittered and pathetic pleading with Nanki-Poo, wins for her the sympathy of the onlookers to such an extent that they turn on Nanki-Poo with the refrain, " If she's thy bride, restore her place ". In the second verse she pours vituperation upon Yum-Yum to such an extent that not only does she lose the sympathy she has just gained, but the crowd fear for Yum-Yum's life, and sing with anxious fear " If true her tale, thy knell is rung ", finishing, as Katisha joins in their singing, on a note of terror. The whole of this phrase must be one continuous crescendo of intensity of feeling, rather than one of tone. In fact, it is not possible to make a great increase of tone, owing to the writing for the voices. Sullivan has deliberately placed the vocal parts in this way, in order that Katisha can dominate them vocally as well as mentally.

After the opening phrase " If true her tale, thy knell is rung, pink cheek, bright eye, rose lip, smooth tongue," the remaining words must be hammered out in strict rhythm, and with increasing intensity to the minims. The tension is relieved by the courageous defiance of Katisha by Pitti-Sing, whose action and song, " For he's going to marry Yum-Yum " restores the courage of the whole assembly, shown when they all sing the lighthearted chorus, " On this subject we pray you be dumb ". This chorus must be given with a gay lilt (6/8), immaculate diction and bright carefree singing.

The company now turns its back on Katisha, who is so affected by the callous attitude of youth to middle-age, as to forget her anger in her overwhelming loneliness. At the end of her brief but lovely song, her old spirit returns and she turns once more with venom upon Nanki-Poo, attempting to unmask him as the son of the Mikado. Urged on by Yum-Yum and Nanki-Poo, the chorus interrupt with their cries of defiance. " Oh, ni bikuri shakuri to ". These interjections must be given fortissimo throughout, and sung with a clearly marked rhythm, alla breve. The first phrase with a long pause, the second and third pauses getting shorter, and after the third interruption (the last one with a pause), the music is sung in strict tempo, with Katisha shrieking her " of your ", and " the son of your " . . . in between the phrases. The first " OYA " with its syncopation, must be clearly marked ff, and the " O " on a semi-breve, must be attacked forte; then a big crescendo made to the " YA " which must be sung staccato. There should also be a pause on the semi-breve bar.

Katisha now sings in uncontrolled temper, " Ye torrents roar, ye tempests howl ", and is answered with mounting scorn by the company. Great care must be taken to avoid a mechanical performance of this response; the correct verbal stress must be made so that the *meaning* of words is clear, and not just the words themselves.

Non legato
"We'll hear no more, ill omened owl,

To joy we soar despite your scowl,
Legato
The echoes of our festival

Shall rise triumphant over all."

The next response must be sung molto sostenuto —

"Away you go, collect your hordes

Proclaim your woe in dismal chords."
cresc.

The remaining music sung under the voices of Yum-Yum and Nanki-Poo must be piano, and be support only, never obtruding.

The final chorus, " We do not heed their dismal sound " must be sung with a full throated joyful defiance. Triumphant from beginning to end.

We do not heed their dis-mal sound, For joy reigns

ev - 'ry - where a - round   etc.

" THE MIKADO "—ACT 2

No. 1—Girls' Chorus

This is a happy carefree chorus, to be sung with an artless charm and a lilting rhythm. On no account must it be allowed to drag. Take great care that all the semi-quavers are given their exact value and that the intonation and blend of sopranos and altos is impeccable. Pitti-Sing's solo must be sung with a delicate plaintive charm, but not in any way mournfully. Sullivan by his choice of key (G flat) has given the necessary colour to the solo and any further stressing of the mood by the singer will result in a distorted picture.

No. 5 and No. 6—Entrance of the Mikado and Mikado's Song

In these numbers the function of the chorus is first to prepare for the entrance of the Mikado and Katisha, and then to become spectators who reiterate important words sung by the two principals.

The " Miya Sama " chorus must be boldly but mechanically sung, to match the clockwork-like gestures that in such court circles are attitudes of obeisance. Each inter-jection of " Bow, bow," must be sung with firm attack. At the end of each verse of the Mikado's song (No. 6) the assembled company repeat the refrain in a spirit of approval and acclamation. It is important to pay close attention to note values, otherwise instead of $\frac{6}{8}$ ♩ ♪♪♪♪ there will be heard $\frac{6}{8}$ ♩ ♪ ♫♩ which will rob these phrases of their strength. The whole tone from G sharp to F sharp on " Will achieve " is also of paramount importance.

No. 7—Trio and Chorus

Here the chorus have the task of supporting the three principals, Ko-ko, Pitti-Sing, and Pooh-Bah, in their story of the imaginary execution. On no account must the refrains be sung in an unintelligent, mechanical manner. Each verbal phrase must be sung with complete conviction:

> "We know him well,'
> He cannot tell
> Untrue or groundless tales —'
> He always tries to utter lies,'
> And every time he fails.
>
> Her terrible tale
> You can't assail,'
> With truth it quite agrees; '
> Her taste exact for faultless fact
> Amounts to a disease."

In the final refrain when they are singing of Pooh-Bah, there should enter into the voices an undercurrent of sarcasm on the phrase " He speaks the truth, whenever he finds it pays ", and this should be still more noticeable on the repeated " Exactly ", as the chorus make their exit.

In all these scenes with the Mikado, it is vitally important that the chorus keep their minds on the focus of attention throughout. This always means the person who is singing the solo; on no account should the eyes be allowed to wander.

Finale—Act 2

In this brief finale the whole company repeats a short extract from the gay motive in the Act 1 finale. They sing with controlled abandon.

"IOLANTHE"—ACT 1

No. 1—Opening Chorus

It is difficult to find a more delightful opening chorus in any light opera than the one Gilbert and Sullivan wrote for " Iolanthe ".

Deliciously absurd words and music for this self-introduction of the pretty feather-brains; for as Celia says " If you ask what is the function of our never ceasing motion, we reply without compunction that we haven't any notion ".

Properly performed, this opening chorus should have the audience chuckling, after the first few bars, but to achieve this result it is necessary that the fairies themselves have certain qualifications. First, they must be in appearance and in their dancing, " Dainty little fairies ", and second they must realise the humour of the words, so admirably set by Sullivan. Costume, make-up, lighting must all contribute to the scene, and finally the lyric must be sung definitely to the audience.

In order that the humour is to be correctly emphasised in the singing, it is only necessary to adhere strictly to Sullivan's music. With the exception of Leila's solo, all the singing must be staccato, with absolute cessation of sound during the quaver rests. As a result, many words are sung with the syllables detached from each other, thus establishing the character of these charming, non-thinking fairies.

It is essential, but not easy to achieve an exact performance of this opening chorus. The phrases must be rehearsed slowly one by one, until every detail of phrasing is correct. The first word must be broken thus: " Tri—pping ", and not as in the vocal score " Trip—ping ". The slurs on " —dy knows why or ", must be gracefully sung. Watch " We must dance ", so that the " t " of " must " is not omitted.

The syncopation on page 14 V.S., bar 2, must not be allowed to drag. The word " we " must be precisely placed even if the second syllable of " whither " is clipped short. The crotchets and minims must be given their full value, but sung non-legato.

In Celia's solo the alternative notes, on the last line of page 15, should be taken, and also in bars 1 and 2, on page 16. In the third bar of page 16, on the words " Haven't any " the second and third crotchets should be respectively G and A, and not two D's as printed. This is according to Sullivan's MS, and is the version now sung by the D'Oyly Carte Opera Company.

Leila's solo, the words of which show the sentimenal side of the fairies, should be sung legato and molto espressivo, at the same time giving an impression of innocence. A slight meno mosso during her first four bars, helps to introduce this change of feeling. The tempo is picked up on " We can ride ".

When, at the end of her solo, the fairies once more sing, they revert to their original " unthinking singing ". A charming effect can be obtained if on page 20 the words " Entrancing, most entrancing " are sung molto legato, and with a joyous rapture.

No. 2

In the scene preceding this chorus, the fairies show themselves as creatures of feeling in their plea for Iolanthe, and their singing must be sincere and warm. The refrain " Welcome ", etc., must be sung joyously and with a warmth of " welcome ". Each individual fairy must show a personal happiness in the return of a much beloved and sorely missed friend, if this scene is to be convincing. Do not allow the tempo to flag.

No. 4—Exit of fairies

The ever-young fairies in bidding farewell to Strephon, must show in their singing and general mien, an interest that is " un-aunt-like " towards their charming nephew. There must be no dutiful intoning of the two phrases " Fare thee well attractive stranger ", and " Aye call us and we'll come to thee ", but they must be sung with a coquettish warmth. This gives place to their original mood on continuing with " tripping hither ", etc.

No. 6—The Peers Chorus

For general remarks see page 7.

The singing throughout this chorus requires a noble, round tone and great attention to phrasing and rhythm. Each note must be given its full and exact value, and each verbal phrase its correct rhetorical stress. Mechanical wooden singing is to be avoided. Each verbal phrase needs careful study, in order to achieve the best result.

" Loudly let the trumpet bray." Do not allow any cutting short of the notes; let the phrase be sung molto sostenuto with every consonant articulated carefully. The accompaniment of horns will, by reason of the instrumental phrasing, add precision to the vocal phrase.

The " Tan-tan-tara "s require a brilliant incisive tone accented " Tan-tan-tara; the first " Tan " being sung with enormous impetus and the " Ra " sustained for a full minim.

" Proudly bang the sounding brasses ", the same accents as the opening line. All " Tzing boom "s sung rhythmically and non-legato.

"As upon its lordly way, This unique procession passes:"   Start this phrase *p*. e molto legato crescendo to " lordly " with a slight stress on " lord ", then continue without a break "this", etc., which phrase must come over clearly and patronisingly to the audience. The following reiterations of " Tan-tan-tara " require to be sung very rhythmically with a steady crescendo to the last " Tan-tan-tara, Tzing boom " which must be hammered out fortissimo.

Now the tenors sing with aloof disdain " Bow, bow, ye lower middle classes ". A clean attack is needed for each " Bow " and the words " lower middle classes ", " Ye tradesmen, bow ye masses ", need to be crystal clear but not forced. The repetitions of these phrases by the basses are most effective, if a feeling of scornful dislike is evident. The heavier voices will help in this, but both tenors and basses will have to be drilled in this vocal characterisation before a good result is obtained. The secret lies in the mental picture within the minds of the singers; the disdainful tenors should have raised eyebrows and a bland expression, whereas the scornful basses will have lowered brows.

The " Tan-tan-tara "s following should be sung as before molto crescendo.

Now the tenors sing softly and molto legato, with utmost conceit, " We are peers of highest station ", with the basses eventually joining in with their staccato phrases in quiet agreement with the sentiments expressed.

Where tenors and basses join in three part harmony, the phrases require to be sung with a firm rhythm, with the quavers on "lower middle classes" and " tradesmen, bow ye masses " all stressed firmly. There is often a tendency, even with the best choruses, to hurry or slur over these passages, but by marking the rhythm as suggested above, this danger can be avoided.

Make certain on page 45 V.S. that Sullivan's dynamics are strictly observed; then an exciting climax can be obtained. The passage for tenors:—

"Tantara, ta ta ta ta ta ta (Repeated four times)

Tantara, ta ta, Tantara, ta ta (Repeated once)

Tantara, ta ta ta ta ta ta ta"

will be unhurried and rhythmic, only if it is accented thus. I advise that singers " cheat " or " stagger " the breath marks: that is for each person to snatch a breath when necessary so as to avoid all snatching a breath at the end of a phrase. In this way a really good crescendo can be built. The chorus then have time to breathe before the final " Bow, ye lower middle classes . . . " *All* the " Tan-tan-tara"s with which this number finished, should be sung with a strong accent on the " Tan ". On the first line of page 48 V.S. these accents will fall on the weak beats of the bar, and in conjunction with the strong beats in the orchestra, they will sound very exciting.

No. 7

The short reiterations by the Peers at the end of each verse of the Lord Chancellor's song, are almost casually sung, but, as always, with clear diction.

No. 8

The first phrase by the Peers should be sung piano, or better still mezza voce, with true meaning on the words " rapture ", " beautiful ", " gentle ", and " dutiful ". These phrases must convey to the audience the impression that Phyllis has made upon the Peers.

The refrain to the following verses, sung by Mountararat, Tolloller and Phyllis, must be sung mezza voce to give the impression that the Peers are just thinking out loud.

No. 9

The reply " No, no, indeed high rank will never hurt you " should be sung with a feeling of reassurance, as well as of disagreement with Phyllis's remarks.

No. 10

The first refrain to Tolloller's song which follows, echoes a note of dismay, and the second refrain is one of despair.

No. 11

Here the Peers' attitude is of amazement at being turned down for a mere shepherd; which attitude gradually turns to one of haughty anger. As they leave the stage, they recover their aplomb and return to their disdainful attitude toward mankind.

No. 13—Finale Act 1

The first interjection by the Peers should be sung in the manner of male gossips lighting upon a possible bit of scandal. Although the words must be clear, do not allow them to be clipped. Each dotted quaver must be given its full duration. The second interjection " We heard the minx remark . . . " is delivered slightly louder than the first, conveying shocked surprise on the part of the Peers.

A little while later, when, in reply to Strephon's statement " This lady's my, mother " the tenors sing " This lady's his what ? ", do insist that, in spite of the surprise conveyed, the words are *sung not spoken*. I am of the considered opinion that unless specially asked for by the composer, deliberate speech, as opposed to quasi parlando, is an anachronism in a musical ensemble. Note too how Sullivan has, by means of a leap of a sixth, given the musical picture of surprise. So too should the laughter of a few bars later be *sung*, as Sullivan indicates. I know that in both these cases, speech is sometimes used in the performances, but it is not consistent with good style. Of course with ill-trained singers speech is the easy solution!

On page 85 V.S. the Peers echo the Lord Chancellor's sentiment " Had this refreshment been denied . . . " Here is an excellent opportunity for gently underlining their kindly stupidity, for, although Strephon is taking Phyllis from them, they are sad at the thought that he might have died, had it not been for his mother's care. The phrase must be sung softly (basses, if you don't watch them, will bellow it), and with genuine feeling. If there is any idea of codding, the result is just amateurish and bad. Mountararat explains to them their mistake, and they agree with him.

If all these interjections are to make sense, the Peers must in the first place, take an intelligent interest in the action. In other words, their focus of attention must be accurate.

A few bars later, now that Phyllis has spurned Strephon, the Peers sing " Oh, Rapture ": another place where true feeling is necessary, and not just a loud sound. A small climax is built when they sing " Not a word, you did deceive her ". This must be sung indignantly, with an increase of tone on the second " you did deceive her," giving a cumulative effect on the minim.

After the exclamation " To which?", etc. (to be sung, not half-spoken), the Peers regain their natural conceit, and sing in a completely self satisfied manner " Lucky little lady ", etc. There must be a feeling of smug pride in the phrase, " Yes, Countess, Countess, the title ". In the final phrase of this section " But of what, I'm not aware ", see that the quaver rest is scrupulously observed, and the repeat of the phrase sung sostenuto.

The fairies on entering, must sing with all the crispness evident in the opening chorus and it must be quite clear to the audience that they have come to give assistance to Strephon. When Strephon begins his explanation of his problems, the Peers interrupt with expressions of disapproval. Here again it is very important that the quaver rest after " Oh fie ", is observed, otherwise the exclamatory nature of the words is lost.

The " tarradiddle, tarradiddle, tol lol lay " must be accented thus:

The same remarks apply to the fairies' interjections, except that the first remark " Oh Fie, Our Strephon's not a rogue " must be sung angrily with a strong accent on " Not ".

When the fairies and Peers sing together on page 96 V.S., in order to get clarity of performance, accent thus:

Basic rhythm

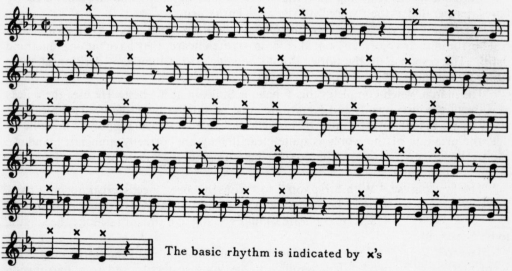

The chorus on pages 98 and 99 V.S., in which the fairies and Peers sing the same melody in octaves and double octaves, needs careful preparation. First the singers must understand and appreciate the basic rhythmic pattern within the quaver phrases.

The basic rhythm is indicated by **x**'s

These accents are not so much to be sung as felt by the singers, who will then have a definite rhythmic framework upon which to hang this long succession of quavers. Having grasped this framework, any gabbling of words or notes is then automatically avoided. At the first rehearsal of this passage, each section of the chorus must sing the phrases slowly, until the notes are accurate. Then with the chorus master clapping the rhythmic pattern given above, the phrases can be sung with increasing speed, and in a surprisingly short time an accurate, clean and crisp performance can be achieved. Not forgetting the molto crescendo.

Although I have sometimes heard a slight stringendo in the last few bars, I feel this is unnecessary to achieve a brilliant climax. The strange vocal colour of the basses and contraltos in their lower registers, is a most charming and unusual effect: so don't allow any indifferent work from these sections. Also don't allow over vocalisation in this chorus, as this will not only blur the diction, but rob the singing of its forcefulness.

After the Lord Chancellor's unfortunate remarks, the fairies sing (page 101, V.S.) their disapproval of his attitude and choice of phrase, in a highly indignant manner. No matter how accurately the notes are sung, if there is not a feeling of strong indignation, the action will sag and become dull. Furthermore, there will be no preparation for the amusing phrases sung by the Fairy Queen, immediately after.

The Fairy Queen is then topped by Phyllis singing " Should they launch terrific thunders . . . ", and finally the fairies, Peers, Phyllis and the Queen join to complete this section, in music of increasing intensity. This crescendo must be carefully controlled, and in order to be fully effective, must start piano, as Sullivan marks (page 103 V.S.). The crotchets at bottom of page 105 V.S. must be hammered out with equal accent and increasing intensity. Phyllis and the Queen must be able in their sustained notes to top the music with a ringing fortissimo. The climax is reached finally on the last bars of page 107 V.S.

The Fairy Queen now discloses her identity and the Peers, in shocked voices sing, in a tone of amazement " We never knew we were talking to an influential fairy ".

The " Into Parliament " chorus calls for nothing more than neat singing and diction. A touch of comedy is to be marked, when the Peers, bad at spelling, sing " P A-arliament " as if asking how the word should be spelt, and are answered by faires exasperated at their stupidity " P A R—Parliament ".

After the " curse " is given by the Queen, the Peers must sing " O Horror " with real horror in their voices, and not as if, as is so often heard, they have sat on something sharp. The response by the fairies should be sung with triumphant derision at these cowardly mortals.

The march which completes this Finale, is Sullivan at his best. He uses the voices as if they were instruments and every note must be sung as he wrote it. This means in many cases, that the words must be broken, and verbal phrasing ignored. In spite of this, the meaning of the words is quite clear if they are correctly enunciated, and the chorus singers do not allow the counter-marching to take their attention from the dramatic situation.

The first phrase " With Strephon " to " consequence " needs crisp opening bars, the semi-quavers as short as possible, and a crescendo of intensity from " opens out " to " consequence ". The second phrase should be sung in a similar fashion; the singing to be non-legato.

The following phrases are to be sung in a like fashion until the fairies sing " the word prestige is French ". This requires to be sung sostenuto and in a patronising manner, poking fun at these irate Lords. The following phrase " Although our threats you now pooh-pooh " is once more non-legato.

On the change of key page 119 V.S., the Peers seem to recover their normal poise and sing softly, but with supreme confidence and assurance " Our Lordly style you shall not quench with base canaille ". The interruptions from the fairies must be as in joke, but when the fairies commence threatening once more, " Your Lordly style we'll quickly quench ", etc., the Peers interrupt with approbation at the sound of these foreign phrases from the lips of mere girls.

Once more they join in singing about Strephon (page 121-R.) and a climax is now to be built up to the end of the music. On " We will not wait, We go sky high ", the fairies must sing with clear ringing tone, sustaining the minim to its full extent, and giving a slight crescendo. The Peers sing at the same time, " You needn't wait, Away you fly " non-legato, until the top of page 123 V.S. where the tone is sustained whilst keeping strictly to the rhythmic pattern.

During the remainder of the march, each note needs to be sung exactly as written, with the precision of a first-class quartet of brass. A crescendo is necessary in the quaver passages preceding the tied minims, and this last page, if it is to be effective, should be sung with the greatest intensity of all.

" IOLANTHE "—ACT 2

No. 2

The fairies must enter singing with truly gay excitement, making it quite clear that they have avenged themselves for the insults and insolence of the Chancellor and the Peers. Strephon, their protége, is now all-powerful in Parliament.

The quavers in the first bar should be sung with equal stress so that the words are quite audible, and the remainder of the lyric phrased thus:

The Peers sing their verse in an irate manner, so that Leila's remark at the end of the number " You seem annoyed " has reason. The phrasing follows: the general pattern of the fairies' verse.

Although this chorus is not a musical high-light of the opera, great care should be taken over the points mentioned as it is essential dramatically that the meaning of the lyric is made quite clear to the audience.

No. 3

The short refrain to each verse must be sung each time on a rising tide of patriotic fervour and pride and with complete sincerity. The most must be made of every word and the vocal tone be rich and noble.

No. 4

In this number the fairies, both soloists and chorus, are in a flirtatious mood but the coquetry of the words must avoid interfering with a charming vocal line. No quasi parlando is to be tolerated, but the final words " don't go " may be spoken.

No. 5

The four bars sung by the fairies require sincere singing and a smooth, round tone. Don't let the altos use a harsh chest voice on the final " I wonder ".

No. 11

In this scene, which includes number 10, the light-hearted gaiety of the opera gives place to tragedy, the full significance of which must be clear in the minds of the company if the performance is to be worthy of the situation. The fairies, off-stage, in singing " Forbear, forbear " are pleading with Iolanthe not to break her vows and incur the penalty of death. The " Aiaiah willaloo " is sung as a lament. There must be a constant increasing of the feeling of sadness, mingled with fear and horror of the doom which awaits Iolanthe at the hands of her Queen. It reaches a climax at the beginning of the last phrase, which, starting forte, dies away to a pianissimo.

At " H " make certain that the " aiaiah "s finish on a quaver, and a slight glottal shock at the end of the word helps portray the feeling of despair. Every " Willahalah " should have a tiny crescendo to the " ha " and then decrescendo.

No. 12—Finale, Act 2

This is a light hearted waltz and, sung as such, ends the opera on the right note of gay fantasy.

No. 1

The scene opens with the contadine, each making a posy of red and white roses. As they work they sing to tell the audience that these posies will bear a message of pleading to those for whom their hearts are aching. This chorus must not be sung sadly but with a gay flirtatious air. The singing of the opening words " List and learn " has been dealt with in detail in Part I, pages 2 and 3, and must be a gentle but firm demand. Great care must be taken in the phrasing, nuance, and rhythm, not forgetting beautiful tone. At all costs the audience must hear the final consonants in the phrase " White and Red ".

N.B. bars 11 and 12, page 9 V.S. *no* sliding from one note to another.

When Fiametta sings it is understood that there are only two men for whom the maidens sigh. With sadness they sing " They, alas, are only two ".

In order that this opening scene is a logical preparation for what follows, there must be a Latin gaiety underlying the sighs and the pleadings. Don't let the singing be profound. In the following scene, the gondoliers are told that although Marco and Guiseppe will have first pick, there will still be enough girls for the others!

It is Antonio, with his song " The merriest fellows are we " who establishes the character of the gondoliers. This song with its rousing chorus of Tra la's must be sung with a swaggering bravura, the rhythm of the chorus hammered out with all vigour possible. Quavers and crotchets are sung exactly as written; the rests meticulously observed. Only when the " Tra la's " are sung as written in the E flat section is the section correctly phrased.

The phrases of welcome on page 23 V.S. sung upstage, must be cleanly delivered and the words audible. Let it be clear that the girls are offering their " love, homage and duty ".

As Marco and Guiseppe enter they begin a flirtation with the girls, and are joined in this by all the gondoliers. It is essential that this mood is borne in mind, otherwise the scene will become dreary. All must sing gaily and lightly; especially the men. Stress the interplay when the men call the contadine " Signore " and the girls reply " Gondolieri carrissimi, siamo contadine ".

For translation see appendix C.

If the meaning of the words is understood, and the flirtatious attitude maintained, the scene is charming; correct phrasing and nuance will follow automatically, and the stage will remain alive.

Then comes the duet between Marco and Guiseppe, to which all listen with attention; the girls because they are entranced and the men in the hope of picking up a few hints.

Marco and Guiseppe next discuss how to choose their brides. Correct phrasing and syllabic stress when the chorus reply (page 38 V.S.) will not only keep the scene alive, but avoid any possibility of these phrases sounding mechanical.

The next interjection is one of excited anticipation (page 39 V.S.).

When the chorus complain that the two gondoliers are trying to cheat, they do so with mock anger, at the same time joining in the joke. There should be laughter in their voices. Such characterisation of music does not interfere with rhythm or clarity of words. The section should end with a crescendo (page 41 V.S.).

The Nursery rhyme (page 42 V.S.) should be sung allegro moderato, with even more laughter in the voices.

When the brides are caught, and the chorus sing " Rapture, rapture " and " just

the very girl he wanted ", watch, especially in the second phrase, the syllabic stress.
Avoid an equal stress on all the syllables and phrase thus:

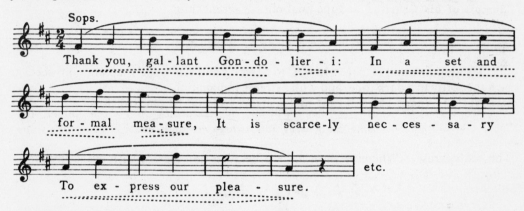

Just the very girl he wanted

Page 47 V.S. Accent the entry of the chorus thus:

Tra la   la la la   la   Tra la la   la   la____

The extra accent on the 3rd beat bar 3, adds strength to the phrase.

When rehearsing the next section (pages 48-50, V.S.) take the sopranos first and do
not play the 3/4 accompaniment. This will ensure that they sing equal crotchets and
that there is no suggestion of a 3/4 rhythm. Next insist on a musical phrasing. Although
Sullivan has put no phrase marks, I cannot believe that he intended a mere mechanical
pointing of the crotchets, irrespective of the verbal sense or the characterisation.

Sops.

Thank you, gal - lant Gon - do - lier - i: In   a   set   and

for - mal   mea - sure,   It   is   scarce-ly   nec - ces - sa - ry

To   ex - press   our   plea - sure.   etc.

The vocal accompaniment can then be sung softly under the melody. The transition passage of Tra la's (page 50, V.S.) will be sung with vigour, preparing for the last
section " Fate in this has put his finger "; this should be sung in four bar phrases
with a good swinging rhythm. The final bars giving a gay au revoir to the audience.
No. 9

This chorus number contains a rhythmic pattern that is continually occurring in
these operas; **6/8** ♪. ♪♪♪. ♪♪ | . This is a difficult rhythm to sing. If a short
time is devoted to a simple preliminary exercise the difficulty goes. Tell the chorus to
repeat several times the word " Amsterdam ", exactly as it is normally pronounced.
It will then be seen that they are speaking in the above rhythmic pattern.

"Am - ster-dam, Am - ster-dam." etc.
6/8 ♪. ♪ ♪ ♪. ♪ ♪

Next have the musical phrase (page 87, line 3, bars 1, 2, 3, V.S.) sung to the word " Amsterdam ". It will then be found that the notes are being sung exactly as written.
Finally rehearse the phrase with Gilbert's words, and all will be well.

Other points to observe are: first, good attack on each phrase, " Bridegroom ",
etc. Second, the dotted minims are to be sustained to the fullest extent. Third, a good

crescendo made on the last bar of page 87, leading to " We in sincerity ", etc., sung molto legato, page 88, line 2, bar 3, attack fortissimo and continue *ff* to the end.

The vocal accompaniment to Tessa's song which follows, needs to be sung very quietly; never obscuring the solo line. The Sopranos only, in " When a merry maiden " etc., page 91, sing espessivo, whilst the other voices sing sostenuto. The final phrase " All is right ", etc., should be sung quietly, but gaily, and with great precision. The accompaniment to the second refrain is only a support for the solo and should be sung as such.

Finale—Act 1

Strong vocal attack and a feeling of amazed questioning is all that is necessary for the opening statement. Make sure that the dotted quavers are fully sustained and the semi-quavers at the end of each phrase are sung with precision. Excellent diction is taken for granted. At " H " stress equally the words "Has anybody blessed" and "Sample of his Charity" and the final phrase accent thus:

"Or have you been adopted by a gentleman of quality."

The response at " J " page 110 V.S. to Marco's and Guiseppe's explanation, needs to be sung softly in a dark tone, and with extreme indignation.

At " O " (page 114 V.S.) the first sentences should be phrased thus:

"Sing high, sing low, wherever they go."

The next phrase " Wherever they go " to be sung non legato, with exact rhythm

etc.

At " P " the ladies of the chorus carry the important words, and in order that these words are completely audible, the men *must* sing softly. I would even advise shortening the crotchets in the men's line to quavers, as this will ensure Gilbert's words being audible. Also I do not feel that these two-part chords need be more than " touched in ", they have little musical significance. At " Q ", all sing notes of similar length which automatically gives the increase in tone which is needed to build towards the climax, " Hail O King ".

Now, from " Q " to " R " make certain that all crotchets are sustained, but without blurring the consonants. Often, in their anxiety about diction, singers in a passage such as this will sing the following:— instead of:— It may be, in the case of inexperienced singers, that the former should be accepted, rather than the diction should suffer. I have allowed a chorus to sing so myself until such time as good diction became a habit. Then I insisted on a more legato line in passages of this character which resulted in exact values of notes without poor diction. Be patient, however, and do not try for everything at once; always allow in early stages, clarity of words to take precedence.

At " R " the music calls for a great increase in tone and fine legato phrasing. Insist too that the music is sung with great sincerity and dignity, especially in " We do not bend the knee "

At Bar 5, 2nd line, page 117 the sopranos only should, after attacking *ff* the first bar, make a diminuendo on " Hail ", so that on the rising interval to the *G* they can make a big crescendo. This is extremely effective and must be followed by a fresh attack from all voices on the next bars " Hail O King ". There should be still a little power in reserve, so that the final " Hail O King " (page 118 V.S.) is the dynamic climax.

It is essential that if the final section (page 124 V.S.) " a la barcarolle " is to be fully effective, it must be sung molto legato in broad sweeping phrases and with joyous anticipation.

Allegro moderato (à la Barcarolle)

The interjections under the four solo voices, need only be sung as written : *P* and detached. No crescendo until page 129, bar 2, 2nd beat, then a quick crescendo leading to the final pages. Once more an increase of intensity is necessary on the final " Then away ", etc., in the last three bars, and a breath must be taken before the final " Away ".

" THE GONDOLIERS "—ACT 2

No. 1

At all costs this opening chorus must be cheerful. If the tempo is allowed to drag the music will sound lumpy. Nor must the performer be too conscious of the bar line; the music must be felt in phrases and not bars. Do not allow the basses (1st and 2nd) to be wooden in their rhythm. They, having a very dull vocal line, must get a " spring " in their singing (see section 1, page 4). All basses are apt to bellow " This form of government ", etc. Stop this at once and insist on a light tone and intelligent verbal phrasing. The final phrase of each section " Tempered with equality " is to be sung with a neat, pointed accentuation.

No. 2

The refrain of this number, is a simple patter refrain. The basic rhythm (See Chapter " The Patter Refrain ") is:—

The first bar of the refrain with " Oh " sung on a *D*, is a danger. Unless care is taken with the vocal quality and the vowel sound, the result is rather as if all the singers had sat on something sharp!

No. 4

Here is the phrasing for this number. The girls must be bubbling over with excitement the whole time and the men reacting to their happiness.

The refrain on pages 154-157 V.S. is a type we have met before. Feel, rather than make, an accent on the 1st and 3rd beats of the bars and let the words come naturally. On page 156 V.S. an accelerando should be started so that on page 157 V.S. the music is alla breve, with the accelerando continuing to the pause on the penultimate bar. Make certain that the last words " about it " are sung as written ♪ | ♩ ♩ 𝄽 𝄽 ‖

No. 5—" The Cachucha "

This is one of the high lights of Act 2, and it should be perfomed with a spontaneous gaiety. Both the music and the dancing must have a joyous abandon which will excite the audience.

The 3/8 rhythm is deceptive in its apparent simplicity and in spite of best intentions the performance can become rigid and dull. It is by careful attention to phrasing that this can be avoided.

The only difficulty with diction occurs on page 159 V.S. " And the clitter, clitter, clatter ". This is extremely difficult to sing at speed and those who cannot manage the " CL " should sing " Kitter ", etc. This compromise is not apparent to the audience and should be accepted rather than have the diction blurred.

In the following example I have given the phrasing which will give the best result from the points of view of music and verbal sense. Make certain the basses and tenors, who have dull lines of repeated notes, also adopt this phrasing. Remember the words

" Wine when it runs in abundance, enhances the reckless delight of that wildest of dances ", and let this be the keynote of the scene.

Tempo di Cachucha

et sim

During the final 16 bars of the cachucha make a steady crescendo to " Dances ".

N.B. The last bar on page 159 V.S. should read " Pitter ", etc., and not " Clitter ".

No. 8

This chorus, sung by the Ducal party, presents no problems of phrasing or diction. Be sure that there is proper pride in the singing throughout.

No. 12—Finale. Act 2

Before one can hope to obtain a performance worthy of this brilliant finale, it is essential that the chorus have a clear understanding of each turn of the drama and the part they themselves take, in the unfolding of the final pages of the story.

In each of their interjections the chorus underline the situation, and for this to be convincing, it is the intelligence with which they use their imagination that counts.

I have listed these interjections below together with the impelling thought.

(1) Page 213 " She will declare ", etc.   Anticipation
(2) Page 214 " Speak woman speak "   Command
(3) Page 216 " Is this indeed ", etc.   Amazement
(4) Page 219 " Then hail O King "   Loyal fervour
(5) Page 221 " Once more ", etc.   Gaiety . . . all's well that ends well

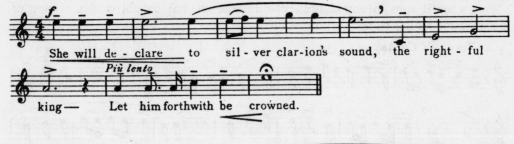

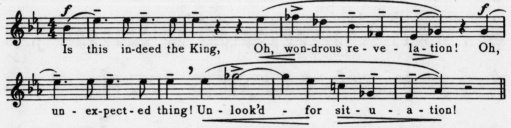

Once words and music have been learnt, the chorus must never be allowed at any rehearsal to forget the feeling with which the above sections are to be sung. Forbear with me when I say yet again, that it is only by constant endeavours on the part of performers and directors that this expression of personal dramatic participation is felt by the audience.

Gilbert's subtitle is "A Slave of Duty". I would like to add in capitals A SATIRE ON THE VICTORIAN MELODRAMA AND GRAND OPERA, for this must never be forgotten throughout rehearsals and performances.

Before beginning rehearsals of this opera the male chorus must have a clear picture in their minds of the complex character of the pirates. They are, as Ruth discloses in the finale, "all noblemen who have gone wrong". They are sensitive—too sensitive in point of fact, to the kindlier side of life. They never attack a vessel weaker than themselves, they always allow orphans to go free, and "life without a touch of poetry in it", would be impossible. To compensate for this sad lack of piratical qualities they assume an exaggeratedly terrifying appearance and mode of behaviour. Unfortunately they never seem to be able to carry out their villainous intentions, as they are always, at the eleventh hour, swayed by a higher moral force. Even their attitude towards the ladies—"We intend to marry your daughters", is surely a trifle unpiratical! In Act 2, they attack the Major General because he lied to them, but how easily is victory snatched from their grasp by the charge to "Yield in Queen Victoria's name".

This is a truly great comic opera with a wealth of comedy in the characters and in the situations.

No. 1.

On page 4 Section 1, will be found details of phrasing and syllabic stress for this chorus. Do not let the indication *moderato maestoso* trap you into a too slow tempo. At (C) page 15 V.S. the change from *f* to *ff* should be marked not only by an increase in tone, but by an underlining of the spirit of celebration. Beware in this chorus of any coarseness of tone or of performance.

No. 3

Vigorous attack on "You are" and a fresh attack on "Hurrah" and similarly on "It is" followed by a fresh attack on "Hurrah for our Pirate King", and again on the repetition, will give satisfying results.

No. 5—Entry of Girls

This chorus should be sung with the dewey-eyed simplicity of the Victorian Miss. Any sophistication of manner or tone is not in character with the scene which follows when Edith, Kate and Isobel chatter of mermaids, and the girls respond with wholehearted abandon to the suggestion "Let's take off our shoes and stockings and paddle". The vocal line is to be lyrical and charming, carrying crystal clear words. Archness is not to be tolerated.

Climb-ing o - ver rock-y moun-tain, Skip-ping riv - u - let and foun-tain,

cresc.

Pas-sing where the wil - lows qui - ver, Pas-sing where the

wil-lows qui-ver By the ev - er - roll-ing riv - er, Swol-len with the

No. 6

Ralph's opening words and the girls response " A Man ", are to be sung in strict tempo. The girls can choose their own reaction so that, according to their individual characters, some will sing " A man " with amazement, some with horror and some even with pleasurable anticipation.

This is not spending undue time on a detail, for it can be a lesson in the value of individual characterisation whilst still working as a team. This personal reaction is to be followed through in the next phrase for the girls chorus, "A pirate! Horror!". This is to be sung with no suggestion of quasi parlando.

The final phrase "How pitiful his tale, how rare his beauty," should again be

sung, not as from a body of people, but as from a number of individuals each expressing a personal feeling towards Frederick.

No. 7

A complete sincerity and an unobtrusive pointing of the responses to Frederick's ingenuous suggestions, is all that is required of the girls in this number.

On page 37 V.S. observe carefully the rests after " Alas ", " Breast," and " Beauty ", but if possible the next phrase " Of making worldly interest subordinate to a sense of duty ", should be sung in one breath. This will need careful attention to breathing! On page 39 V.S. it is the first phrase that should be phrased over " . . . here whose ", etc., and it is permissible to allow a quick breath in the second phrase after " disappear ".

The cry " 'Tis Mabel ", from all the girls, can be sung by each according to her feelings towards Mabel. Perhaps exasperation, philosophic resignation, surprise or positive dislike. In fact their whispered remark that follows Mabel's reproach is very definitely catty and must come over as such.

No. 9—" Poor wandering one "

Apart from the one phrase " Take heart; no danger lowers. Take any heart—but ours " which should be quite pointed, the girls have only a few quiet chords of accompaniment to sing.

No. 10—" How beautifully blue the sky "

This scene is one of Gilbert's and Sullivan's happiest inspirations. Musically the contrast between the inquisitive girls and the idyllic phrases sung by Mabel and Frederick, could not be more clearly marked.

Rehearse music and words separately; i.e., teach the notes on " La " and then make the girls speak the lines in rhythm. The breathing must be staggered (See Section 1 " The Patter Refrain "), so that there is a continuous flow of conversation. The chorus master should obtain finally a performance of metronomic precision together with a clearly enunciated verbal line. When Frederick and Mabel start singing, the girls frankly eavesdrop, and their singing becomes mechanical.

Let the commencement of each section " How beautifully ", etc., be attacked with a slightly exaggerated enthusiasm in the weather forecast, to help mark their apparent indifference to the " goings on " of the hero and heroine.

No. 11

The girls are again shocked by Frederick when he warns them of the approach of the Pirates, " Men who stick at no offences ", and in an agitated manner they agree to leave at once. When they are caught, and they realise that the intention of the Pirates is matrimony they, in truly Victorian manner, become acquiescent. Details of phrasing in this music have already been discussed in Section 1 (page 15), and it only remains to ensure that the Pirates sing with mock severity and the girls with a charming coyness, to bring out the humour of this scene. Do not forget that later, when questioned by their Father, they say, whilst flinging their arms around their Pirates, "Against our wills Papa ! "

No. 12

It is Mabel who recalls the pirates to their senses with her opening recitative, and the pseudo ruffian Samuel says " We'd better pause or danger may befall; their father is a Major-General ". The girls then reply in a hoity-toity manner " Yes, yes, he is a Major General ". There is then a delightful volte face when the Major General enters, cheered by everyone.

It is by bringing out these details of performance that the opera is kept sparkling throughout and the danger of dull patches avoided. Remember Gilbert did not pad out his dialogue but wrote each line with a purpose. Even interjections correctly sung help build the characters of those concerned.

No. 13

The patter choruses in the Major General's song are quite easy. The basic rhythmic pattern of the first (page 63 V.S.) chorus is:

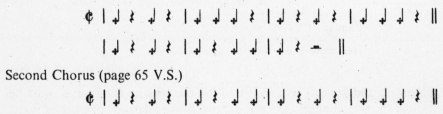

Second Chorus (page 65 V.S.)

No. 14—Finale. Act 1

Unless one remembers that this opera is a *satire* on melodrama, the opening sequence of this finale may be over-played and the performance, in particular that of the pirates, will no longer be " comic " but merely grotesque. Therefore, any crude exaggeration of performance must be stopped at once. Do not allow such interjections as " Poor fellow " to be " codded " and if the men's chorus (page 71 V.S.) " See at our feet ", etc., is sung with beautiful tone and phrasing and with slightly exaggerated pathos, the situation is very funny.

The patter chorus (pages 73 to 78 V.S.) has as the basic rhythm

$$\frac{6}{8} \mid \flat\, \gamma\, \gamma \mid \flat\, \gamma\, \gamma \mid \flat\, \gamma\, \gamma\, \zeta\, \gamma \mid \text{ et simile}$$

Avoid any crescendo on page 76; then the change to *ff* will be electrifying. The strictest attention to diction and note values is imperative. A bar of six quavers must be sung ♪♪♪ ♪♪♪ and not ♪♪♩ ♪♪♩ or ♩ ♪♪♩ ♪♪

In this patter chorus the girls' words are different from those of the pirates. The pirates are doubtful and they sing " *If* he's telling ", but the girls know that their Father " *has told* a terrible story ", and they say so. Make quite sure these different reactions are quite clear to the audience.

The Chorus " Hail poetry " presents no problems to any well-trained chorus and musicianly director. The only dynamic marked is *ff* at the beginning. Here it is quite apparent that, apart from wanting the opening phrase to sound full and rich, Sullivan left the rest to the conductor.

In the 6/8 chorus which follows, do not lose sight of the verbal phrasing and allow the music to become jog-trot. Also during rehearsals, watch the syllabic stress and make sure it is natural.

It is. Hurrah for the orphan boy.

Hurrah for the orphan boy!

Oh, happy day, with joyous glee,

They will away and married be.

Should it befall auspiciouslee,

Her sisters all will bridesmaids be.

Oh happy day, with joyous glee,

They will away and married be.

Should it befall auspiciouslee,

Her sisters all will bridesmaids be.

When Ruth enters and appeals to Frederick, the remarks by the Pirates must be an exact imitation of the interchanges between the two principals and sung accordingly.

The music of the remainder of the finale is an extended version of No. 11. The pirates, however, have now got their wish, and, in their gruff way, they pay court to the girls. Watch the chording on page 92, particularly bars 6, 7, 8, after M where the basses, if not checked, will sing out of tune. Insist on a clean break at bar 9 and a fresh attack on *Divinity*. Do not let the crescendo leading to M develop too rapidly or the climax will misfire.

"THE PIRATES OF PENZANCE"—ACT 2.

No. 1

This moving but simple music with its gently rocking accompaniment sung with warm tenderness, expresses the womanly concern of the daughters for their father. N.B. The final consonants of " Seek " and " Weep " will need very careful rehearsal if they are to be heard.

No. 3

Before any progress can be made in rehearsing this chorus, the " Tarantara's " must be sung correctly. It is ideal if all the policemen can roll their Rs. Usually only a few can.

♪♪. ♪|♪. ♪♪. ♪♪ ʏ |
Ta ran ta ra, Ta ran ta ra

Sung with this accentuation (note accent on last " Ra ") with a quickly rolled R, the phrase comes alive. At letter B a quiet accent on the beat is all that is needed, with a rolled R, of course.

So far the policemen have been very brave about their job, and have sung with braggadacio, but when the girls sing " Go ye heroes—go and die " it is another matter and the " Tarantara "s are more an expression of concern at an unpleasant fate. Be careful that this phrase, although sung softly, is still accented as above.

At letter D the girls phrase is an exhortation and is to be sung as such. " Go, ye heroes, go and die ". To achieve this, insist on a forceful " G " on the word " Go ", also a clear double consonant at " And Die ".

Ten bars after letter E the girls are once more heard singing:

"Go to glory and the grave.

For your foes are fierce and ruthless,

False, unmerciful and truthless,

Young and tender, Old and toothless,

All in vain their mercy crave."

N.B. Don't allow any suggestion of a triplet to intrude. Keep to the rythmic pattern

♪. ♪♪. ♪ etc.

Apart from the opening phrase, these words are badly set for the sopranos who have to sing in their lowest register and are almost inaudible. Even with the help of the contraltos it is nearly impossible to obtain any " bite " in the singing. One must depend upon excellent diction and carefully accented rhythm to make the passage carry conviction. The adjectives " Fierce ", " ruthless ", " tender ", etc., will not be convincing, or perhaps even heard, unless each singer visualises them as she sings. Remember when the policemen hear this passage, they tremble and their knees knock. How can this be a sincere reaction if the girls merely gabble some unintelligible gibberish?

After the Sergeant's next phrases, the policemen pluck up their courage again as he sings " Yes. It's very evident these attentions are well meant ", and they continue to the end with renewed zeal.

During this last section, which is a superb example of Sullivan's genius, Mabel and Edith repeat their solos and the girls fill in with simple chords that add a rich texture to the whole. Ensure that the chords are correctly sustained with the dynamics as indicated in the V.S. and, above all, that the words are sung with complete conviction.

Nos. 9 and 10

The policemen return, singing a short extract from their first song, still with the idea of keeping up their courage. Mabel's remarks about " Death and Glory " and " Duty ", do not help; in fact, quite the reverse, as becomes evident when the Sergeant sings his somewhat lugubrious song. Don't allow the interjections " his employment ", etc., to become too obtrusive or unrhythmical. The undercurrent of bewildered unhappiness should be apparent in the final phrase. Start the " Ah " on the low C rising with a portamento to the B flat 7th each time.

No. 11

When the pirates are heard singing off-stage, the policemen show their terror and run and hide.

No. 12

This number is straightforward and with careful attention to diction and rhythm, is perfectly easy to bring off.

The phrase " In silence dread our cautious way we feel " being sung forte by the pirates, whilst they stump about the stage, may to some observers seem " corny " but, earnestly and sincerely done, it is, in point of fact, extremely funny.

Come friends who plough the sea, Truce to nav-i-ga-tion,
Take an-oth-er sta-tion, Let's va-ry pi-ra-cee
With a lit-tle bur-gla-ree! With a lit-tle bur-gla-ree!

No. 14

In the refrain of the Major-General's song, the music calls for beautiful tone and sensitive phrasing. The first tenors at letter B should sing with a true bel canto. It should be the aim of the directors that this number be a " musical interlude ", then the entrance of the girls immediately after will be fully effective.

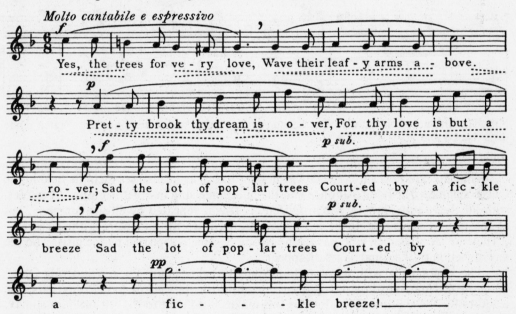

Yes, the trees for ve-ry love, Wave their leaf-y arms a-bove.
Pret-ty brook thy dream is o-ver, For thy love is but a
ro-ver; Sad the lot of pop-lar trees Court-ed by a fic-kle
breeze Sad the lot of pop-lar trees Court-ed by
a fic-kle breeze!

N.B. The 2nd tenors and basses phrase their lines the same as the 1st tenors. The 1st tenors should stand out by virtue of (a) their expressive singing; (b) the quieter singing throughout by the 2nd tenors and basses.

The D'Oyly Carte Opera Company have for many years omitted the second verse of this song. This is very wise, as in its original form the action was held up too long.

At letter C the girls enter and sing a brief patter chorus. Rehearse this very slowly, so that the notes and intonation are absolutely correct. After the words and music are memorised, do not be satisfied until the feeling of startled surprise is fully projected.

The Basic Rhythm of this Chorus is:—

 et sim

The Breathing should be " staggered ". (See Section 1 " The Patter Refrain ").

From this point until letter H, all musical phrases from soloists and chorus are to be sung without any disturbance of the rhythm; the girls with despair, the pirates with triumph, and finally the policemen with despairing courage.

At H the chorus for pirates and policemen is very difficult to perform because of the placing on the stage, and often a carefully rehearsed performance can fail, if the stage business is overdone. When, however, the correct balance between stage business and music is obtained, the result is satisfactory.

N.B. The first note is a quaver. The Second phrase starts with a semi-quaver. Watch tenor divisi bars 8 and 9.

Finale—Act 2

The Sergeant now turns the tables on the Pirates, as he charges them to yield in the Queen's name. They do so at once and the policemen sing in quiet triumph " Yes, Yes, with all their faults they love their Queen ". This is repeated by all the company, but as the pirates are about to be led away, Ruth rushes on and betrays their secret— " They are all noblemen who have gone wrong". This is repeated by the girls, who see any objection to their marriages disappear.

The opera ends with a quotation from Mabel's song " Poor Wandering One " accompanied by the whole company. It is unfortunate that in the closing bars, the tessitura for the sopranos is so low, as this makes it difficult to b.... a brilliant climax. It helps if some of the sopranos take the top A flat on the last chord.

No. 1

The opening chorus of sailors sets the correct atmosphere for this opera. The audience should feel the tang of the sea and the happy-go-lucky outlook of the " Jolly Jack Tar ". It is very difficult to bring this off as the tessitura of the opening music is so low. Do not allow the singers to " sit " on their voices—this will only make matters worse. Lack of vocal volume is to be compensated by crisp, vital diction and above all a cheerful delivery of the lines.

Make certain that the attack on " We " is firm with accurate note values. When the tenors sing " Ahoy, Ahoy ", ♪ ♪. ♪ | ♩, see that the minim is held to its full length with a slight crescendo. The final lines are phrased thus:

> >
"Our saucy ship's a beauty,
> >
We're attentive to our duty,
>
We're sober men and true
≥ > > > < >
We sail the ocean blue."

No. 3

Expressive words sung in a beautiful mezza voce with a quiet sadness, will make the first two interjections " He sang Ah welladay ", a moving echo of the soloist's phrase. Do not be afraid of a true pianissimo. The third phrase " Yes, yes, the lass ", etc., needs a firm but not boisterous delivery.

In the ballad, the repetition by the sailors of " A world of wealth is sighing " needs very careful phrasing and tuning. Rehearse the tenors and first basses until the thirds are absolutely true; then add the second basses. See that the word " sighing " is sung as a sigh. A slight lingering on the initial consonant will help considerably.

The pianissimo chords which accompany the final phrases of the song should be sung mezza voce with a quiet but firm attack. If the pianissimo is really observed, it is possible to give a controlled crescendo on the penultimate chord, resolving on to a chord of C, sung forte.

No. 4

The recitative for Captain and sailors, which opens this number, needs considerable rehearsal before it is correct. The sailors replies must be in strict tempo, and sung with the smartness of the Royal Navy. The semi-quavers should be strictly observed as they add crispness to the phrases. At the same time, do not allow the phrases to be shouted. The last phrase " You do us proud, Sir ", is the most difficult of all. It should be sung non-legato, with a crescendo to the word " proud ".

During the Captain's song, the sailors reply to him in a forthright, but respectful manner. Care taken with the consonants in these phrases will be well repaid in clarity of delivery. Verbal sequences such as: " Right good Captain, too " and " He commands a right good crew ", if rehearsed slowly and thoroughly will bring about a general improvement in the men's diction. Do not forget the note of interrogation in " What, Never? " This is very important, for without it the famous reply " No, never ", " Hardly ever " loses its point. Make sure the phrase " He's hardly ever sick at sea " is sung forte, then the piano phrase which follows is more effective. A slight stress on "hardy" and "Well bred" is desirable, and the last words "Captain of the Pinafore" should be firmly accented.

No. 6

The problem of off-stage singing has rarely a satisfactory solution. In this case, the impression to the audience should be that of an approaching boat-load of girls. This effect can be got by either starting piano and gradually getting louder, or by the girls singing away from the proscenium and gradually turning around towards it. It depends upon the acoustics of the theatre which is the more effective, and should be checked by someone standing at the back of the auditorium during rehearsal.

No. 7

When Sir Joseph's barge is seen with its "crowd of blushing beauty", the sailors forget the formality of the occasion in their pleasure at receiving such charming guests as "the sisters, cousins and aunts", and the opening of this chorus is sung accordingly with a gleeful chuckle in their voices. When the Captain appears (page 34 V.S.) there is a quick crescendo and strict Naval behaviour is once more the order of the day.

As the ladies enter, they bring with them an air of gay frivolity. The opening phrase "Gaily tripping, lightly skipping" is most difficult to sing accurately. Take sopranos and altos separately and slowly until each semi-quaver is sung in tune. Do not be satisfied with a slipshod or hurried approximation of notes which will sound

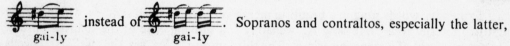 Sopranos and contraltos, especially the latter,

must sing lightly with a bright clear tone. The sailors' remarks must be phrased and sung with a flirtatious gallantry.

N.B. Do not allow the top E in the last bar to be oversung.

Watch the contralto line (page 36 V.S., bars 16 and 18) and insist on musical phrasing otherwise it will sound angular. In the ensemble (page 37 V.S.) keep the baritones and basses piano whilst they gently mark the quaver rhythm.

The unison passage "Ladies who can smile", etc., should be sung molto legato and graciously. The extension on "politely" must exude charm as the singers diminuendo. Watch the tuning of the ladies and tenors. The final phrases need only to be sung as written, with continued charm, to bring this section to a graceful finish.

A final word of warning. Make certain throughout that there are no expressionless or glum faces on the stage. Everyone must be cheerful.

No. 8

In response to the Captain, the company sing three sturdy "Hurrays". Do not allow the quaver on the first syllable to be clipped.

The first response "And they are his sisters", etc., (page 40 V.S.) is sung with great dignity. This is difficult to bring off by the sopranos as the notes lie so low for them. Forceful diction with good attack will balance this weakness of writing.

The second response " And so do ", etc., is one of fine pride.

The third, started by the ladies, has an unpleasant memory of stormy seas but it builds to a vigorous finish. In all of these responses, see that the quavers are sung evenly with clear attack and lively rhythm.

No. 9

In the repetition of Sir Joseph's lines by the company, it is essential to have a clean, unhurried delivery of the words. People habitually repeat some interesting fact that they have heard and it is this element of interest, shown by the chorus, that will keep this scene alive. It is the verbal phrase, carried on a simple musical line, which counts. Watch the notes in " Now he is the ruler of the Queen's Navee ". Do not be afraid of allowing the chorus to get in a gentle dig at Sir Joseph during the last two verses.

No. 10

Unless the sailors begin by visualising in their mind's eye each of the attributes of a British Tar that they list in this number, the performance will never come off.

The sung notes are very simple with the exception of the scale of E major on " fist be ever ready ", etc., which should be watched. It does, however, require considerable imaginative ability to deliver with conviction the phrases " His nose should pant, and his lip should curl, his cheek should flame ", etc. These phrases positively tumble along upon each other's heels. But, as the three principals have comedy business during this refrain, the sailors' performance is liable to be under-rehearsed and therefore under-played. Well done it provides real support for the principals.

No. 12—Finale. Act 1

The chorus enter, anxious to hear from Ralph the result of his proposal to Josephine, and their opening phrases need a crisp excited delivery, but with a well-controlled rhythm. Make certain they sing " What cheer " and not " Wha' cheer ". The " T-CH " is difficult to sing cleanly but it is necessary. When they are told that Josephine has scorned him because of his humble birth, they sing with deep indignation " Oh cruel one ". This they sing twice, so phrase the passage as follows:

Remember that a repeated verbal phrase should never be delivered twice in the same way. This is a bad artistic fault.

After Deadeye's gloating, the sailors sing with rising indignation " Shall we submit? Are we but slaves ", etc. For this to be sung properly each singer must feel a personal slight in Josephine's attitude to Ralph. Don't be satisfied with just forceful singing, go over and over this section (pages 60-62 V.S.) until each individual performance is a true expression of a personal emotion. On page 61 V.S., continue without a breath "Are they but slaves? Shall we submit?" The double consonant " Slave*s*? *Sh*all " will give verbal clarity without breaking the crescendo.

Ralph now prepares to take leave of life and after his sad little solo, the chorus take up the phrases in harmony. The first step towards a moving performance of these phrases is to persuade, or bully, the singers into producing a true piano. This is never easy to achieve, as singers, even if they have the technique to sing piano, seem to love the sound of their own voices! Be firm and do not give way, for after all any fool can sing loudly but only an artist softly! Phrase this section as follows and, once more I say, be sure it is sincerely sung:

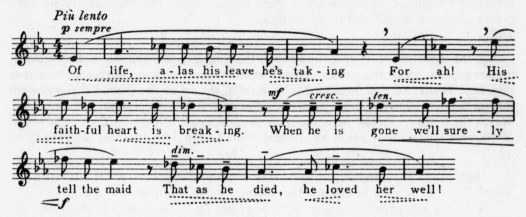

When Josephine appears and sings " Ah, Stay your hand, I love you ", the chorus repeat her words with urgency, for Ralph now holds the pistol to his head. In the next phrase " Yes, Yes, she loves you " the chorus confirm the good news.

The principals now sing of " joy and rapture ", with Deadeye prophesying trouble, but when Josephine and Ralph start to plan their elopement, the chorus join in the conspiracy. Do not allow this music (pages 71-72 V.S.) to be anything more than quietly spoken thoughts; the principals, singing piano, should still be quite audible. On page 73, let the sopranos only sing with Josephine and give the altos Hebe's line until the word "none" on page 75. The sopranos line needs to be crystal clear in notes and diction, and not too loud. The remaining voices, if not checked, will sing *mf* instead of *pp*. The crescendo to the *ff* passage must not start earlier than indicated; in fact, I prefer to make a clean change of dynamics with no preliminary crescendo. This is most effective. In this *ff* passage let an accent be felt on the first quaver of each beat. Then the singing will be firm and unhurried. All the words must be easily heard and understood by the audience. Check from the back of the circle at rehearsals.

After Deadeye's final threat, the company must fairly spit out the words " Back vermin ", etc. (page 76 V.S.).

All now break into a swinging 6/8 chorus in which they express their delight at Josephine's action. Keep a good springy rhythm going throughout this section. Then they sing in praise of the British Tar and the instructions given on page 51 for No. 10, hold good here. Keep the excitement going without sacrificing rhythm or diction and the finale will finish on a triumphant note.

Do not forget that if these changes of mood are not definite, the finale will be flat and tedious.

" H.M.S. PINAFORE "—ACT 2

No. 18

This is the elopement, and the sailors enter singing pianissimo in a conspiritorial manner. Make sure that the notes are sung detached as Sullivan intended. In their relief at Deadeye's explanation of the sudden noise, they forget their purpose and sing

" It was the cat ", legato and forte. This happens once more on page 116 V.S.

When the Captain makes his presence known and chides Josephine, the sailors angrily sing "Now hark", etc. This reaction of the sailors prepares the way for Ralph's and Josephine's defiance of her father which reaches a climax in the phrase " He is an Englishman ", which must be sung with great pride.

The Bo'sun then takes up this theme in his song which follows, and it is with proud defiance that the sailors repeat the refrain " For in spite of all temptations", etc. Here is another case where volume is not to be mistaken for sincerity; each sailor must mean what he sings and if he does, this will show in his stance and demeanour as well as in his singing.

When the Captain says his famous " damme ", the chorus ejaculations are much more effective sung than spoken. During Hebe's solo, which follows immediately, the chorus phrases " He said damme " are a murmured undercurrent, but need most careful rehearsing before they are accurate.

Sir Joseph sends the Captain to his cabin and the company repeat the words " This is the consequence of ill-advised asperity ". Have this phrase sung softly in one breath and in strict rhythm with a ————— ————— on the second bar. Everyone is shocked. During the remainder of this number (pages 129-130 V.S.) see that the indications strinendo molto, sempre stringendo, and vivace, are observed with discretion. The feeling of indignation should be very marked and the refrain " For he is an Englishman " with which this section ends, requires at all costs full rich singing with firm vigorous attack on each phrase. Do not allow the chords to be sung detached or non legato. Keep a legato line in addition to this attack. Let clearly articulated consonants clarify the change from one chord to another, and not a cessation of tone, no matter how brief.

No. 19

When the chorus join the principals in singing " For crime unknown ", etc., page 133 V.S.) do not allow a forte entry. Keep to a piano and do not allow the attack on " For " to be vigorous. The audience should not be aware of any immediate increase in tone; then the crescendo at the end of the phrase will be most effective. The phrase " How terrible", etc., (page 135 V.S.) is a quiet expression of horrified amazement and must be sung firmly but softly.

No. 20

Unless the chorus listen to Mrs. Cripps with intelligent attention, their responses will be meaningless.

The reactions are as follows:

1. Alarm—" Now this is most alarming ", etc.
2. Interest—" Now this is the position ", etc.
3. Disgust—" However could you do it ", etc.
4. Amazement—" The one was Ralph, our brother ", etc.

If these reactions are remembered, the phrases will sing themselves. Watch that the quaver rests are observed and in no circumstances allow " A many " to become " Ah! Many ".

No. 21—Finale. Act 2

This consists of quotations from previously sung numbers and contains no new problems. There is a point to remember, however, in the refrain " For he loves little Buttercup" (page 147 V.S.) see that it is sung in two bar phrases, thus avoiding a " tumty-tum ", monotonous performance. Now that the girls have got their men, all can show a touch of sentiment in their singing.

No. 1

For a brief resumé of the plot of " Patience ", see Section 1, page 6 " The Thought Behind the Words ".

As Lady Jane says " There is a transcendentality of delirium—an acute accentuation of supremest ecstasy—which the earthy might easily mistake for indigestion. But it is *not* indigestion—it is aesthetic transfiguration! "; and this is what all the maidens are suffering from since they met Bunthorne. In their singing and posturing there is always the " supremest ecstasy "; a reaching towards higher things, rather than anaemic resignation to worship from afar. If this is forgotten by the performers, the opening chorus ceases to be amusing, and becomes just dreary.

The singing of this chorus is not difficult, but keep it moving at all costs. The accompaniment is very monotonous and will become stodgy if taken too slowly and the singing will then drag. Always take " Twenty years hence we shall be twenty lovesick maidens still," in one breath.

No. 2

In the few short phrases that the maidens sing, their reactions, though brief, are definite. The sopranos sing with incredulity " Most marvellous ", the contraltos with disapproval " and most deplorable ". During Patience's gay song they sing with envy, and disapproval, " Yes she is blithe and gay " before the final " Ah miserie ".

No. 3

With the entry of the Dragoons all this aesthetic nonsense is forgotten and the audience is brought face to face with the world of action. A good martial delivery with no frills is required here. Again I give warning that the officers must sing and not, in an excess of enthusiasm, bellow. A good round forte with no forcing of tone, together with incisive verbal attack will be enough.

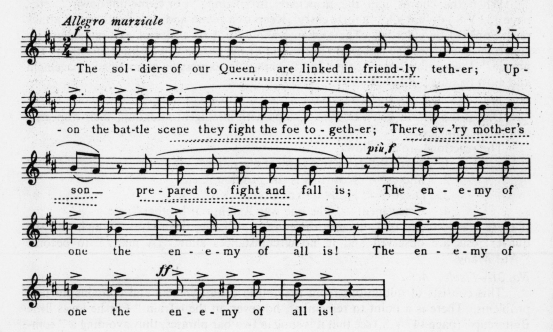

The vocal accompaniment to the Colonel's song needs to be sung as indicated—pianissimo—with crisp rhythm.

No. 4

Bunthorne enters, followed by the lovesick maidens singing a plaintive chant. The phrasing is very important if a wooden performance is to be avoided.

The Dragoons sing with intense irritation at the spectacle of their ex-fiancees' rapt adoration of the effeminate poet.

The maidens give vent to their feelings after Angela's solo, with exaggerated pathos.

Bunthorne betrays his cynical attitude towards his posing, in his opening remarks, the closing phrase of which is repeated by the Dragoons. Although Bunthorne sings with a certain amount of rhythmic freedom, the Dragoons must enter and sing in strict rhythm.

Saphir sings next, giving the maidens another opportunity of showing their feelings. Again Bunthorne betrays his cynicism and again the Dragoons pick up his refrain, but this time continuing with their own complaints. The maidens join in and the number finishes with a double chorus.

No. 5

The officers feel insulted by the attitude of the ladies and show their annoyance as they sing the refrain of this song. Providing the syllabic stress is right, correct note values will follow automatically.

No. 9—Finale. Act 1

The maidens enter leading Bunthorne in chains of flowers. They have shed their plaintiveness, for Bunthorne is going to raffle himself, and they are all going to buy tickets. They sing with an anaemic gaiety, untainted by any worldly feelings.

N.B.   (1) Make certain that the " ND "s of " sound " and " bound " are clearly heard.
(2) When a phrase ends with a crotchet, see that it is fully sustained.
(3) Do not allow a breath to be taken between bars 8 and 9.

A steady tempo is essential throughout the whole of this section.

The Dragoons march on, and in a kindly manner ask Bunthorne what is happening.

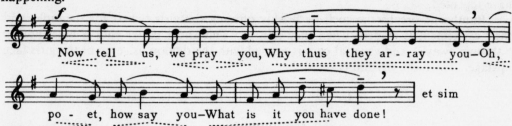

He tells them of the impending raffle, and the maidens, slightly smug, repeat the news as if scoring off the Dragoons, who react with sudden anger. Bunthorne's solicitor is alternately blessed by the maidens and cursed by the Dragoons.

If this section is to flow smoothly, there must be no breaking of the rhythm between the girls' and men's remarks. At rehearsal, have *all* the voices sing *all* the music so that they can feel the continuity. Then allow them to sing only their own lines. The contrast between the blessings of the maidens and the curses of the Dragoons requires to be strongly marked.

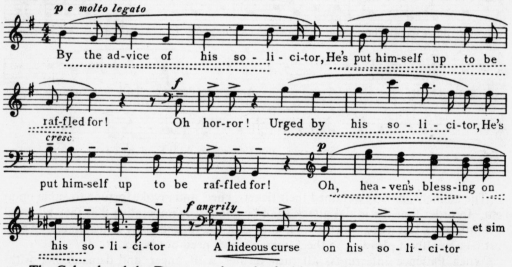

The Colonel and the Dragoons then plead with the girls to return to them. They sing with a desperate urgency.

Next the Duke makes his appeal to the girls and so softens their hearts that, when they repeat with the Dragoons " Our soldiers very seldom cry ", etc., it seems as if they have repented.

Bunthorne breaks the spell by briskly offering the girls tickets for the raffle, and their excitement is evident when they join in. This short patter chorus must not be " thrown away ", and especial care is needed with the diction as some of the girls face upstage. The basic rhythm is:

¢ | ♩ ♪ ♩ ♪ | ♩ ♩ ♩ ♪ | et sim in two bar phrases

The Dragoons now take on a devil-may-care attitude, showing complete indifference as they sing of their rejection by the maidens.

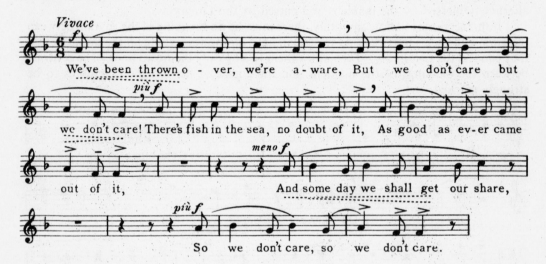

The maidens, having obtained their tickets, kneel and invoke fortune to smile upon them. In order that the initial attack shall be good, it is imperative that they all kneel on Bunthorne's last word " Prize ". If they don't, a ragged entry is inevitable. There must be a wealth of pleading in their singing which need not be too loud.

When Patience interrupts, all turn on her with anger and demand her withdrawal. This is the first time the maidens drop their aesthetic pose, and, properly sung with vixenish attack from them, backed by haughty indignation from the Dragoons, the effect of this passage is electric.

The first phrase to be sung molto sostenuto with increasing intensity. The second phrase to be declamatory with a crescendo to *ff*.

After Patience has explained her presence and offered herself to Bunthorne, the indignation turns to threats. Once more they all order her away.

Patience explains the unselfishness of her love for Bunthorne and, as this is in accordance with the maidens' views, they accept the inevitable and return to their old loves, the Dragoons.

Then is heard the famous sextet " I hear the soft voice ". There is an ever present temptation to take this slowly which destroys the charm of the words and music. The mood is one of happy reconciliation, warmed by the re-awakening of love. Let the performance, above all else, be tender. When the chorus enter it must be with a magical pianissimo, gradually mounting to an expressive forte; the singing flexible, but avoiding any obvious rubato, and the verbal phrases gently stressed.

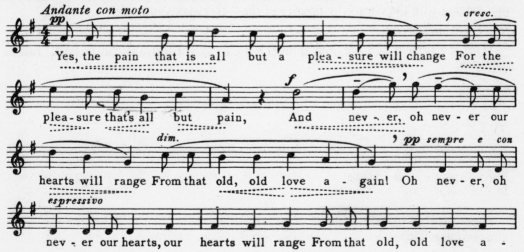

Do not allow the words "change" and "range" to be clipped. Make sure that an unhurried final consonant is heard in each case.

When Grosvenor appears, the maidens turn once more from their Dragoons. (See Section 1, page 4). After he has introduced himself as yet another aesthetic, the maidens in a frenzy of rapture exclaim " Then we love you ".

The finale ends with the maidens surrounding Grosvenor, offering their love with a surprising lack of inhibitions, while the Dragoons rage in the background.

Sing all this alla breve section in broad sweeping four bar phrases, paying strict attention to the rhythmic pattern and maintaining a firm legato line. Do not allow, in the anxiety of singing an accurate rhythm, a jerky staccato performance. Build steadily towards an exciting climax on the penultimate chord.

<h2 style="text-align:center">" PATIENCE "—ACT 2</h2>

No. 3

Grosvenor enters followed by the girls who have discarded their " lovesick ecstasy " and are now tenderly pleading with him to beguile them " with a gentle smile, with a glance of sad perfection ". There is more resignation in their attitude to their new love than they showed when Bunthorne ruled their hearts, and this is evident in the calm poise of their singing.

No. 4

In this song the maidens' lines need only a simple clarity. Insist on " Why ", and " Wheedle " and not " Wy " and " Weedle ".

No. 10

When the metamorphosis of Grosvenor occurs, the maidens follow suit and enter singing with the cheerful vulgarity of the " everyday young girl ".

No. 11—Finale. Act 2

This is a version of a previous quintet with a straight-forward chorus part. Just a gay romp.

No. 1

The curtain rises on the " Corps of Professional Bridesmaids " singing in praise of Rose Maybud. The music is gay and charming, and the lyric gives a delightful picture of Rose whilst also drawing attention to the fact that she is unmarried.

First of all make certain that the girls' voices are divided, so that well-balanced three-part harmony is heard. Do not forget that the fisher-girls, usually the heavy contraltos, take part in the singing as onlookers. Be careful of the moving quavers on " Rose is queen of maiden-kind "; see that the notes are clear and the singing graceful. Each verbal phrase is an exercise in imagination so that the singers project the descriptions quite clearly, but delicately.

> " Fair is Rose as bright as May Day;
> Soft is Rose as warm West Wind;
> Sweet is Rose as new mown hay—
> Rose is queen of maidenkind! "

Sing the third and fourth lines in one breath. Sing the remainder of the lyric in two four-bar phrases, ending on a definite note of interrogation.

No. 2

The first interjection by the girls " This sport he much enjoyed ", etc., can with advantage be cut. The girls are horrified by the story of the curse and they sing in subdued tones the closing bars of this number.

Nos. 5 and 6

It is with great gusto and excitement that the girls welcome Richard.

Do not allow them to oversing their phrases at the end of each verse of Richard's song. Concentrate on a light tone together with complete unanimity of words.

No. 9

In this scene the bridesmaids are hopeful that at last their professional services will be required and they ask anxiously " Oh tell us pray, what doth the maiden say? " finishing with their " theme song ", " Hail the Bridegroom ", etc. As they have sung this many times before, their performance is pretty, but stilted. With each repetition in the scene which follows, it becomes more and more mechanical.

No. 12

When the " Gentlemen from town " arrive, the girls are once more their charming, but demure selves, and they sing their greeting.

Rehearse sopranos and altos seperately at first, until a clear vocal line is obtained without any portamento as the notes rise or fall by a large interval. There are a dozen such pitfalls in the opening section. The musical phrasing is in accordance with the verbal sense.

The gentlemen's answer is very difficult indeed to sing well. First the notes should be rehearsed very slowly until they are exact and not approximate in intonation and value. This is best done by omitting the words and substituting " la " on each note. When the words are added, be careful that the note values remain accurate and a bright 12/8 rhythm results. The foregoing is the groundwork. Now the section has to be sung expressively.

In their attitude towards these village beauties the men are above all things gallant, and they sing their praises accordingly. Do not allow a heavy tone as this will not only destroy the feeling of the scene, but will prove that the singers are not using their imagination; gallantry, even if insincere, is always charming, and loud singing is not charming. Therefore, the next step is to sing the words and music mezzoforte and slowly, so that there is time to think of the meaning of the words and to give an intelligent performance. Correct syllabic stress (see Section 1, page 2) need not mean a distortion of note values, but if all syllables are equally stressed, the verbal meaning is lost. Finally the section can be taken up to speed. Be careful that the last phrase " Your slaves, for the moment, are we ", is sung with a beautiful tone and graciously.

The girls' reply to this declaration by the men, presents similar problems which can be dealt with in the same way. Watch the contraltos when they divide on " But never a lover for me ". Make sure that their line is audible. When the men sing " Then come Amyrillis, come Chloe, come Phyllis " see that this is a request and not a demand.

Do not, when the girls and men sing together in the final section of this number, allow the individual characterisation to become lost, or the difference in rank to become blurred, through over-enthusiastic choral singing.

No. 13

Sir Despard now appears and sings his song of warning, to which the company listen with the closest attention, replying realistically.

No. 15—Finale. Act 1

This finale begins with the bridal procession of Rose and Robin. There is no dramatic action during the number and the value of the scene rests solely upon the beauty of the singing. This happy music is very simply written and needs clear, but unforced, pointing of the verbal phrases.

Then follows the madrigal which in my opinion is the finest that Sullivan ever wrote. The happiness heard in the preceding music now becomes a bubbling-up of rapture. The picture of the four seasons should be reflected in the phrases, " Spring is green—Summer's rose—Autumn's gold—Winter's grey ".

N.B. Any loss of pitch during this unaccompanied refrain can be attributable to one of two causes:

A. Insufficient support for the voices due to faulty breathing.

B. A badly sung scale of G by the sopranos—bars 5 to 8. This latter fault may be due to a combination of bad breathing as well as a faulty ear.

Bars 1 to 4. The crescendo marked in the soprano line indicates a delicate verbal stress to the words " *Fade* " and " *End* ". The other voices must remain subservient to the sopranos.

Bars 2 and 4. Be careful that the top D for the basses is well covered and sung lightly. Otherwise it will be too heavy and destroy the balance of the chord.

Bars 5 to 8. The answering quaver passages in alto and tenor lines must flow smoothly, and the beginning of each group of quavers firmly attacked.

Bar 9 onwards. The descending passage for sopranos and altos should be sung non legato and very gaily, continuing to the end of the refrain.

Bars 14 and 15. *Carefully tune* the 4ths in soprano, alto, and tenor lines.

The drama begins when Sir Despard enters and denounces Robin. The company sing with amazement " Oh wonder ". A clearly articulated initial consonant on " Wonder " and a sustained vowel with the " n " sounded just before the second syllable, gives the necessary effect. The accusations " Ah. Base one " are hurled at Robin with scorn at his deception. When Robin further admits his guilt, the chorus unobtrusively repeat his words.

During the vivace section, the passage for the company should be accented thus in order to be rhythmically and verbally clear:

He'll tell tar - ra - did - dles when he's a bad Bart!
On ve - ry false fid - dles he'll play a bad part!

To mor-als sen-ten-tious a - dieu with good grace   A - dieu with good grace to his

mor als, his mor-als sen - ten - tious!

The basic rhythm for the next 16 bars is:

$\frac{6}{8}$ ♩ ♪ ♪ | ♪ ♪ ♪ | ♪ ♪ ♪ | ♪ ♪ ♪ | ♪ ♪ ♪ | et sim in four-bar phrases

Do not permit too great an increase of tone early in this section. The increase must be gradual, so that the last three bars, sung fortissimo, are the climax. The words "Die traitor" directed towards Richard when he admits his treachery, must be sung with frightening intensity.

At the end of Robin's explanation of his conduct " Within this breast ", etc., he has regained the sympathy of the company and with a complete volte face they acclaim his actions.

It is never easy to ensure accuracy of note values in this chorus. Insist that the dotted quavers are held as long as possible before singing the following semi-quavers. Do not allow any staccato singing to intrude, and broaden the last phrase "Immediately obeyed".

Rose now forsakes Robin and offers herself to Sir Despard to the delight of the bridesmaids who sing their ditty prettily, but mechanically. This they repeat twice more, as the occasion arises.

The final section of the jig sung by the chorus is a gay piece of nonsense requiring the utmost agility of tongue and lips in order that the words be neat and rhythmic. In bars 7, 8 and 9, allow the tenors to give a discreet accentuation to the notes on the first beat of these bars and make sure that the notes of " Embraces his bride " in bars 10 and 12 are correctly detached.

" RUDDIGORE "—ACT 2

Nos. 2 and 3

In these two numbers the girls have a brief refrain to sing in this rhythm:

$\frac{6}{8}$ | ♪. ♪♪♪. ♪♪ | (See Section 2, page 35). Watch the final consonants on " bright ", " tight ", " slight ", and " light ".

No. 4

Choose your best eight singers (four tenors, two baritones and two basses) for the opening of this number which is sung by the " Pictures " only. First-class blend and intonation is essential for, situated as they are on the stage, they can rarely hear the accompaniment. The tuning of the chords for the baritones and basses is very difficult and any uncertainty will completely spoil the music. The final phrase, sung in unison, has a flattened seventh (C natural) in the scale and this requires careful rehearsing before the result is satisfactory. Do not allow the dynamics to rise above a *mf*.

When all the ghosts appear and sing " Baronet of Ruddigore ", the volume will increase by sheer weight of numbers and let this suffice for the moment so that when necessary a good crescendo can be made. The scene is one of increasing terror on the part of Sir Ruthven at the threats and sneers of the ghosts. They must remember this during the whole of the time they are on the stage.

If the singers have difficulty in remembering the " names " they call Robin, and this is very difficult, suggest they write them out a few times. This usually does the trick.

Build to a ringing fortissimo on the last phrase " Set on thee his grisly hand ".

It is with sardonic humour that they sing in imitation of Sir Roderick " We spectres are a jollier crew than you perhaps suppose ".

No. 5

In the few notes that the ghosts have to sing at the end of each verse watch the " Ha Ha "s. Be sure they are sung ♪ ♪ and not ♪♪.

No. 6

Sir Ruthven has yielded to the threats and the ghosts show their approval in a friendly manner. There is, however, still that undercurrent of sardonic humour of which a glimpse was shown earlier on, for whilst graciously asking Robin's pardon, they still threaten him with death if he withholds it. Make this point quite clear by a marked contrast of tone and demeanour in the two words " Or die ". Their response to Sir Ruthven's " I pardon you " is very much " the smile on the face of the tiger ".

The scene ends with the eight pictures singing the closing lines as they return to their frames. Once more, all that is necessary is a soft blended tone and immaculate intonation.

No. 11—Finale. Act 2

The finale as used in the present production by the D'Oyly Carte Opera Company is a repetition of the jig in Act 1.

"YEOMEN OF THE GUARD"—ACT I

This opera is the one incursion into serious realms that Gilbert and Sullivan made, and it is in no way a "comic" opera. There are, of course, moments of comedy but, whatever Gilbert's original intentions were, the story becomes one of unrequited love, with its attendant tragedy.

From the musical director's point of view, this is a satisfactory opera to conduct. The music is beautiful and of great variety, and there is no stylised business to impinge upon the musical sequences.

There is little movement for the chorus, thereby throwing the onus on to the individual chorister to keep the scene alive by his reactions to the drama. It will also be apparent as one reads through the score, that the reactions contain no subtleties as in satire, but are straightforward.

No. 2

In this double chorus, it is impossible to have a well-balanced chorus of citizens unless the tenors and basses are augmented, as the chorus of Yeomen absorbs the majority of the mens' voices. In the citizens' chorus Sullivan has used the voices as if they were instruments and the writing is unvocal, but this detracts little from the brilliant effect if the music is correctly sung. The indication is staccato but do not take this to mean that every note is to be detached. The implied direction is for every note to be attacked vigourously but with no loss to the verbal sense. The chorus parts are duplicated in the orchestral score; the orchestra playing with true staccato.

The scene opens with the citizens singing a song of welcome to the Yeomen as they enter and it is sung with a feeling of pride in the glories of their honourable tradition. In the last phase "Each a bold, a bold contributory", give an accent on the second "bold", as if hammering home the point.

The Yeoman, before they start rehearsing, should have in their minds a definite picture of this body of ex-sergeant-majors and N.C.O's, who have done their term of service and in full stature of maturity have been appointed to this famous guard. They sing with smooth, warm tone, of the contentment attained after years of soldiering.

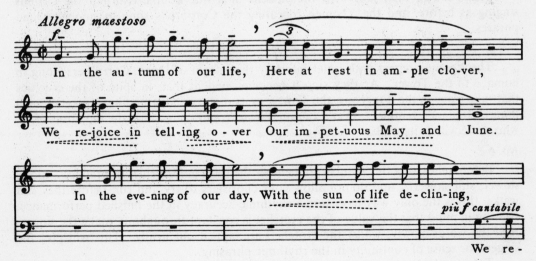

67

At the end of the Corporal's song, the Yeomen show for a brief moment that they are still ready and capable of taking up arms again. Let this be sung with a parade ground fierceness for, once a Sergeant-Major, always a Sergeant-Major!

The Yeomen then join with the citizens in a fine double chorus; the citizens singing as before, and the Yeomen repeating the Corporal's song in smooth broad phrases.

No. 3

The Yeomen repeat with quiet intensity the refrain of Dame Carruthers' song in homage to the Tower. As they sing it becomes evident that, in spite of the cruelties that take place in the dungeons, the Tower, in its dignity and strength, transcends such things. It stands sentinel " O'er London Town ", and commands the devotion of all who serve within its walls.

No. 6

Before rehearsing this number, remember the three golden rules of practice " Slow, slower, still slower ", and do not allow your choristers to try and run before they can walk; this is the only way to ensure a rhythmic accuracy in the finished performance. Bearing in mind that the value of the crotchet is constant throughout, make the singers *read* the words slowly, whilst the crotchets are tapped out firmly. This will give the singers the sense of continuity in the rhythmic phrasing.

Take particular care that there is no deviation of speed in the 5/4 bars or 3/4 bars. When a correct reading has been achieved, then is the time to start teaching the notes and not before. The dangerous bars are when 4/4 alternates with 3/4. There is always a tendency that the last crotchet of these bars will be clipped and, consequently, the next bar started a little too soon.

When rehearsing up to speed, conduct the 4/4 bars in alla breve time (2 beats) and beat out the crotchets in the 5/4 and 3/4 bars.

Finally, the singing whilst strictly accurate in time and diction, should convey the noisy excitement common to crowds in every age.

No. 7

The sopranos repeat the final refrain, accompanied by quiet sustained chords from the rest of the chorus. There is always a tendency to shorten the first of the quavers on " Misery me, lackaday dee ", and this should be checked. Make certain also that the last bar is sustained correctly, with no diminuendo.

No. 12—Finale. Act 1

Before a really first-class performance of the opening section of this finale can be obtained, each chorister must be " Bloody, bold and resolute ". On the stage, the Yeomen are standing some distance from each other, and they will lack the assurance that is given by close contact with one's fellow-singers. This is a time when they have to rely solely on the conductor's beat for attack and ensemble; therefore, at final music calls, place your singers in their stage positions.

The fanfare-like phrases with which the Yeomen address Sergeant Meryll, require to be sung with martial precision.

In the music with which the Yeomen greet Fairfax, it is important that the 2nd tenor line is sufficiently strong to produce a well-balanced triad. If this is not the case, the music, in spite of vigorous singing, will sound thin.

Leo-nard Mer-yll! Leo-nard Mer-yll! Daunt-less he in time of per-il!

Man of pow-er, Knight-hood's flow-er, Wel-come to the grim old Tower;

To the Tow - er, wel - come thou!

After this " official welcome ", the scene becomes less formal and the Yeoman, as it were, " stand easy ". With kindly approbation they respond to Fairfax's modest deprecation of his reputation. These phrases need to be sung with the confidence resulting from thorough rehearsal and with great attention to attack and phrasing.

'Tis ev - er thus wher - ev - er val-our true is found, True

mod-es -ty will there a - bound

The remarks of the 1st and 2nd Yeomen are repeated by the others with additional emphasis. It should be noted here, that in the present performances by the D'Oyly Carte Opera Company, a cut is made from page 81 V.S., 11th bar to the allegro in F major on page 83 V.S. Without this cut the scene is too long.

In the next delightful scene between Fairfax, Phoebe and Wilfred, the Yeomen, as onlookers, pass a couple of remarks to Fairfax, confirming in each case words of Wilfred's. Do not allow the first of these " Aye, he speaks the truth, ' Tis Phoebe " to misfire through bad attack and ensemble. The second " Be thou at hand to take those favours from her ", is to be sung in one phrase, legato and espressivo.

When Wilfred hands Phoebe over to the care, as he thinks, of her brother, the Yeomen, with kindly thought at this happy reunion of a devoted brother and sister, repeat the instructions " From morn to afternoon ", etc. After Fairfax's acceptance of this welcome responsibility, the first stroke of the funeral bell is heard and frivolity stops.

All take their places in preparation for the execution. The music for this funeral scene is very simply written and consequently any faults of performance, in balance, intonation or ensemble, will be exposed to the audience. Balance and intonation can be rehearsed at the same time; men and women separately. Passages containing fourths and seconds need special care. The altos and tenors should also be rehearsed together, for bad chording is often due to these two parts being badly tuned.

Next get the note values correct. The subdivision of the crotchet in the opening phrases must be checked carefully, so that the semiquavers are exactly right. Then make certain that in phrases such as " bell begins to " the quavers are not shortened.

The final check is at the ending of the phrases. All the singers must sing the final consonants of " co*mes*, doo*m*, blo*ck*, to*mb* ", etc., together.

After these details are correct, the chorus can now think of performance. Singing with bowed heads is not enough. The solemnity and tragedy of the scene, if not felt by the singers, will not move the audience. The plea for mercy must be sung with all their hearts.

When the chorus join in Elsie's prayer, allow the altos to sing the opening two bars a little louder than the rest. This gives support to the solo line. (On page 97 V.S., 4th bar, the last note for the altos should be F not G). Build this section to a strong climax in both volume and intensity of feeling.

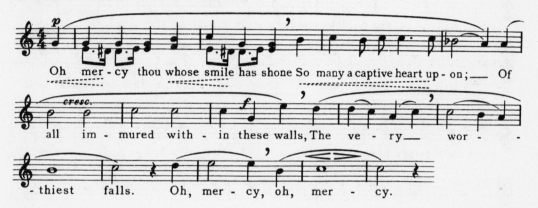

N.B.   In the two long phrases do not allow the taking of a breath to break the shape of the phrase.

When the escape is discovered, the chorus cannot believe their ears, and say so!

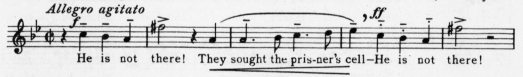

The girls next show pleasure at the escape as they sing " Now by my troth the news is fair ", etc.

The next section "As escort for the prisoner ", etc., will have to be rehearsed a great number of times, until notes and words are clear. The last four bars are particularly difficult. The basic rhythm is:

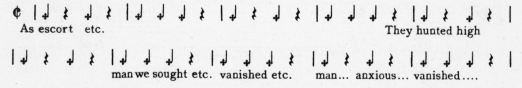

The closing section " All frenzied " is preceded by a sustained " Ah " for the girls only. Don't start this too softly. The full chorus enter fortissimo, with the citizens singing, almost hysterical with excitement, and the Yeomen singing with controlled anger.

N.B.   The florid passage for basses to be sung with a fine legato and steady rhythm.

The divisi of "A Thousand marks" differs from that in the V.S. but gives a better balance.

" YEOMEN OF THE GUARD "—ACT 2

No. 1

The girls sing the opening music calmly until the phrase " Shame on loutish jailor folk—shame on sleepy sentinel ", which is sung angrily at the Yeomen. After Dame Carruthers' solo, they repeat the closing words with derision. Mark the quavers strongly and don't forget the sforzando in the " Pretty wardens are ye, whom do ye ward ".

The Yeomen then sing of the search they have made. All the semiquavers need great precision when sung, and see that all the consonants are clearly heard. The girls interrupt with their words of derision, and as they repeat the opening music, the Yeomen in short phrases agree with the criticism of their work.

No. 6

A shot is heard and Sergeant Meryll and the Yeomen hurry on to the stage followed by a crowd of excited citizens.

As the Yeomen take up their positions, they sing with vigorous tone and a questioning manner, asking the reason for the shot. They must be in their positions at least a bar and a half before they are due to sing; if not the attack will be ragged.

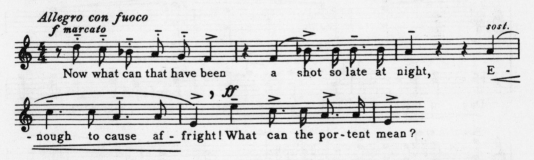

The citizens then join in asking questions. In the few bars before the entry of the Lieutenant, each syllable should be sung with a crisp attack and the canon cleanly outlined. Additional stress is wanted on the last " What danger is at hand ".

Wilfred and Point now explain the reason for the alarm. All listen intently. The chorus join in occasionally as they stress the important features of the story. These interpolations must be a spontaneous reaction by enthralled listeners. They need not be sung very loudly but the enunciation must be clean.

The chorus become very excited at the argument as to whether " it is stone or lead ", and they sing quicker and quicker as their excitement grows.

Be careful not to allow the chorus to run away in this scene. Insist on a perfect ensemble with every word in the stringendo being completely audible.

Wilfred, now a hero, is carried off shoulder high with the chorus acclaiming his deed in triumphant tones.

No. 10—Finale. Act 2

The girls enter in a bridal procession for the marriage of Elsie and Fairfax. Don't let them forget that this is a happy occasion. They must sing light-heartedly and tenderly. Keep the music flowing gently.

Such phrases as " Brave is the youth to whom thy lot thou art willingly linking ", should be sung as a personal tribute to a gallant bridegroom, and with happiness that such a one is going to marry Elsie. The closing phrases " Take him, be true to him ", etc., are sung as a kindly admonition.

After the trio for Elsie, Phoebe and Dame Carruthers, the full chorus sing of the joy that is to be Elsie's.

Then comes the Lieutenant with what appears to be tragic news for Elsie, and the whole company react with moving dramatic phrases, sung with heartbreaking intensity.

bride? Day of ter-ror! Day of tears!

ff

N.B. The opening phrase for sopranos sung molto legato is supported by chords sung non legato (but just as sincerely) by the remainder of the voices.

Take especial care that the phrasing which is rarely the same for all the voices, is observed and it will add a reality to the performance. *E.g.* bars 4 to 7 the girls express their feelings in " Day of Terror " differently from the men who have anger in their voices. Hence the different phrasing.

As Fairfax, speaking as the lawful husband, claims Elsie, the chorus sing with resignation " Thou art his own, alas, he claims thee as his bride ". Eventually, Elsie realises that the Leonard she knows is really Fairfax, and the chorus echo their feelings in the words " With happiness their souls are cloyed " in ringing joyous tones, which reach a thrilling climax on " Joy day unalloyed ".

Jack Point enters and the "joy day" is forgotten. In hushed tones the chorus reply to his " I have a song to sing, O ", and at the end of his verse they sing the refrain softly, as they grieve for the poor broken jester.

Elsie then breaks in with " I have a song to sing, O ", and the chorus answer her firmly. She sings her verse and the chorus repeat the refrain softly at first and then with increasing tone. The singing ends with a series of extended " Heighdy "s. These closing pages need full throated delivery with each " Heighdy " attacked with precision, the utmost vigour and steadily increasing intensity to the end of the final chord.

Throughout " Yeomen ", except in a few scenes, Gilbert and Sullivan are in serious vein. They are not the subtle, witty partners of the " comic operas ", but are intent on creating a tale of human emotions in a sombre setting. For this reason this opera is easier to perform because it requires " feeling " rather than intellectual byplay. The emotional changes must be painted in broad full-blooded style, and the singing felt with intensity, inner fire and purpose.

No. 1

This bucolic chorus marks the prelude to the wedding, as we are told by the singers, of Alexis Pointdextre to Aline Sangazure.

Sing the opening section in D major with greatest possible impetus helped by strongly marked consonants, both initial and final, and allow no decrescendo on any long note. Breath after " sound ", " abound " and " lay ". Sing the last phrase " And from your throats pour joy today " with a cresendo and firmly marked quavers, ending with a forceful " joy today ".

The G major section needs to be sung with a lighter tone, in a conversational, gossipy manner; the men cutting in on the remarks of the girls. Don't allow the gossipy feeling to be lost, but get a little touch of proud singing into the phrase " And that pride of his sex is ", etc. Watch the A in the men's line or it will be flat. On the transition (page 9 V.S.) back to the opening subject, divide the sopranos and altos thus:

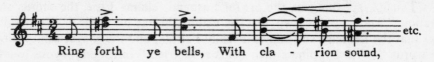

The contraltos D sharp must be full and round and perfectly tuned with the F sharp. Remember, although this passage is sung with vigorous attack, there must be a further increase on " Ring forth ", etc., in the recapitulation.

The passage in octaves needs a smooth legato, and an excellent blend of all voices. The basses will have to be watched, or they will be too loud. In fact all will tend to oversing here if not checked.

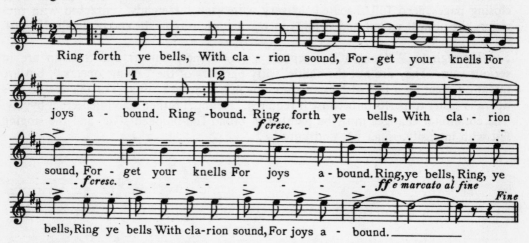

Phrase the build to the end, as shown in the previous musical example. Do not allow the air of excited anticipation to flag at any moment during the opening chorus.

No. 5

As they sing, the girls must express the personal warmth they feel for Aline. Let the opening phrase be sung with true rejoicing at another's happiness, and rehearse the phrase " Lovely Aline " until they really mean what they say.

Each of the following phrases requires a subtle change in feeling and they will well repay thoughtful rehearsal:

> " May their love never cloy,
> May their bliss be unbounded!
> With a halo of joy,
> May their lives be surrounded ".

No. 8

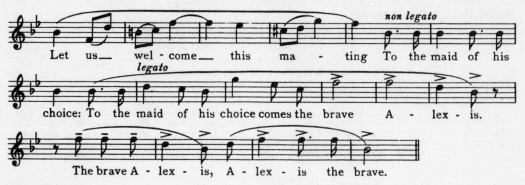

No. 10

Do not allow the singing of this opening section to become " churchy ". Remember it is a cheerful occasion. Maintain a good legato line in all voices. Do not allow any lessening of tone during the dotted crotchets, nor any break before the quaver which follows.

The final section on page 36 V.S., should be phrased thus:

Then follows a fine double chorus in which both men and girls sing a combined song of welcome.

No. 13

This incantation scene needs vigorous attack, in *pp* as well as *ff* passages, and strict attention to rhythm. A touch of demoniacal singing should be given only on the " Ha ha's ".

No. 14—Finale. Act 1

The dramatic pivot upon which this finale turns, is the transformation of each individual personality, from village revelling to trance-like exaltation, as the love potion takes effect.

The opening of this finale " Now to the banquet we press ", etc., is the typical gay 6/8 chorus, and, given a good springy rhythmic performance, presents no difficulties to the singers. Make certain, however, that the rhythmic patterns are clearly defined; especially phrases such as:

"Now for the muf - fin and toast."

Do not allow the quavers to be sung unevenly.

Page 58 V.S. when the sopranos sing their sustained E on " Eggs " and " Ham ", do not allow them to overpower the melody sung by the tenors and basses.

On page 61 V.S., when the whole company sings " None so knowing as he ", etc., take care that the phrase " At brewing a jorum of tea " is sung as written. If not watched they will sing equal quavers throughout the bar. The whole section should be sung in a spirit of joyful anticipation of good fare.

The chorus first feel the effects of the potion on page 68 V.S., when the men sing " Oh marvellous illusion ". These phrases, should be sung thus :

p. 68 V.S.

p. 72 V.S.

When notes and phrasing have been learnt, it is vital to the story, that the sense of bewilderment turning to illusion, is fully realised in the singing. This depends solely upon the ability of the chorus-master to awaken the imagination of the singers.

Remember, *no* vocal tricks! (Ref. Section 1 page 4(c)).

" THE SOCERER "—ACT 2

No. 15

Before the music of the " awakening scene " (page 83 V.S.) can be rehearsed, the chorus-master, or if he cannot, the stage director, should settle the strength of dialect that is to be used and give a clear demonstration to the chorus. The printed word is not, in this case, a reliable guide, as the dialect as printed is not consistent. " Why " should be written " Whoi ", " Rise " " Roise ", " Quite " " Quoit ", and so on.

Having settled this problem the music can now be rehearsed. Insist on a quiet conversational approach, with an air of bemused bewilderment. The fact that the phrases for the men and the women are unison, means that even a mezzoforte is quite heavy. There must also be a strong flavour of the country-bumkins coy courtship, but this must not be overdone. Just an aroma of cows and clover.

When the music changes from common time to alla breve, if the indication " $\sum$ = $\sum$ before " is strictly obeyed, the rest of this section will sound very hurried. Let the speed of the alla breve be governed by intelligent verbal delivery. This will give a steadier tempo than the one indicated.

The music should not sound foursquare or mechanical for after all this is a proposal scene!

No. 16

The two short interjections are expressions of impatient exasperation and are to be sung accordingly (pages 89 and 91 V.S.).

In the ensemble (page 93 V.S.) " Oh joy! Oh joy! ", mark the polka rhythm neatly with correctly sustained dotted crotchets. Allow no crescendo for the first eight bars, but make a sudden change on the ninth bar, from *p* to *ff*.

On pages 95 and 96 V.S., observe carefully the three phrases " Oh joy, Oh, joy, Oh joy ", the first two *p* and the third *pp*. Then clean attack and sustained chords to the end.

No. 22

In this ensemble, the chorus enter fortissimo on page 123, "Oh, what is the matter", etc. The singing expresses a horrified astonishment at Alexis' attitude to Aline. Let every syllable be hammered out in strict tempo, at the same time giving an additional accent thus:

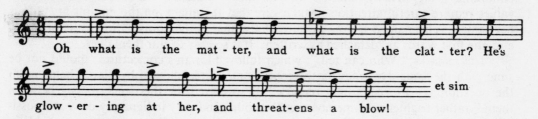

The climax on page 124 V.S. needs all the power, consistent with good tone, that can be obtained from the singers. The tension must be maintained to the end of the number.

No. 24—Finale. Act 2

This consists, in the main, of a repetition of the "Eggs and Ham" chorus and, once more, is sung with cheerful revelry. There is, however, just before this, a passage which is most difficult to sing correctly. (page 128 V.S.).

Do not allow the first phrase to be sung too vigorously by the men. Mark it "con amore", and insist upon warmth of tone rather than quantity. The reply by the girls, "Beloved boy", is espressivo. Then the men sing more warmly "Ecstatic rapture", with true rapture in their voices. The setting of the final response by the girls, "Unmingled joy", is one of Sullivan's least happy thoughts. The top A is almost unsingable to any but the most accomplished singers. It takes quite a time to rehearse this phrase and make it acceptable. Carefully sung consonants: "Un-mingled", will help considerably and, with the strong voices, insist on a covered tone. Let the lyric sopranos carry this phrase with discreet, blended, support from the others.

No. 1

When the curtain rises the members of King Hildebrand's court are discovered in a state of great excitement. They await the arrival of King Gama and his daughter, the Princess Ida, who are late; the courtiers are wondering what has delayed them.

It is, therefore, with a feeling of anxiety they sing " Search throughout the panorama ", etc. This is another of Sullivan's " staccato " choruses and the note values require careful attention. Make sure that the attack on the minims at " Ida is her name ", is firm and decisive. Be careful also that in the phrase "Some misfortune ", etc., the first words are detached as written. It is so easy to slur them over.

The remarks " Who can tell ", which follow Florian's conjectures, should not be sung with the same dynamics on the repetition. Forte followed by piano, helps point the questioning. Florian's final remark " If so there'll be the deuce to pay between them " rather frightens the members of the court, and they indignantly deny the possibility, singing " No, no, we'll not despair, we'll not despair ". Accent every syllable in this phrase and increase the tone on the last " We'll not despair ". See that the crotchets on " No, no ", are not clipped. Start the next phrase " For Gama would not dare " etc., piano with a crescendo to the word " Dare ", and let there be shown a feeling of terror at the thought of trouble and its consequences between Hildebrand and Gama. The remainder of this chorus is a repetition of the opening section.

No. 2

King Hildebrand, in this song, gives instructions for the reception of King Gama. In the first verse it is presumed that Ida has accompanied her Father and all is well. There is an air of cheerful anticipation of the good time coming.

Do not let the opening phrase for the chorus be in any way staccato but maintain a good legato line, together with a springy rhythm. On page 11 V.S., check the second bar so that the quavers on " Give him a cheer " are exact. The same point arises on the " Hip, hip, hurrah's ". Phrase the remainder thus:

Ex. A

In the second verse, instructions are given if Gama has been found to have broken his word. Whilst the musical phrasing is exactly the same, the spirit which prompts the singing is one of gleeful, but spiteful, anticipation at punishing Gama.

No. 4

This is a welcome to Gama's three sons, and it is sung to the music of the first section of the opening chorus.

No. 5

After the three warriors have explained themselves, the chorus takes up the refrain (page 23 V.S.) "They are men of might. Ha, ha", which they sing with approbation. The warriors have, in fact, inspired the members of the court with their war-like outlook, and the courtiers respond accordingly. The words and notes are sung with the utmost vigour and fervour. Do not allow the "Ha, Ha"s to be sung, they must be spoken. Also on page 24 V.S. "Order is obeyed", "Order comes to fight", see that the end crotchets are not prolonged. The long phrase on "fighting" should be sung broadly with a round, full but not forced tone.

No. 6

The final phrases for chorus are an expression of amused amazement.

No. 7—Finale. Act 1

In the opening of this finale, Gama suggests to Hildebrand that if he approaches Ida with due humility "she may deign to look on you," and the courtiers repeat the injunction "Humbly beg, and humbly sue", etc., as a gentle reminder.

Ex. B

But Hildebrand replies to Gama in threatening words. The members of the court repeat his threats, but with the bland smile and exquisite courtesy of a diplomat delivering an ultimatum. This makes the menace of the words "We will hang you, never fear", all the more terrible. The phrasing is the same as in Ex. B.

N.B. In the refrain of the second verse after the words "We will hang you, never fear", the following phrasing will better point the situation and the words.

Hilarion then interrupts and suggests that there is a better method of waging war on women, for, "Nature has armed us for the war we wage". His method is that of Cupid !

This ensemble needs sensitive musical and verbal phrasing of the highest order or else it will become foursquare and jogtrot. The difficulty lies in the parts for altos, tenors and basses. These vocal lines are uninteresting and however charmingly the melody is sung, if the harmonic lines are not equally well phrased, the ensemble will be spoilt.

N.B.   The verbal phrases need only the most gentle of stresses as marked.

To mark the parenthesis, a break of a split second is necessary between the words "heigh-o-let" and "or".

Bars 6 and 7. On the rising passage for sopranos insist on a lightening of the top notes on "urbanity and vanity".

The soprano line should just predominate, by virtue of the other lines being sung a little softer than piano. When rehearsing, suggest that the accompanying singers listen to the soprano line. This will help keep a correct balance.

The syllabic stress should be delicately underlined and each phrase made to conjure a picture in the minds of the audience. The sustained chords on page 35 V.S. should be sung pianissimo. Watch the tuning of the tenors and first basses.

Do not allow any crescendo on the phrase "Oh dainty triolet", page 35 bottom line, bars 2, 3, and 4. The change to forte must be deliberate. On the 2nd bar of page 36, sing the "O" of "violet" on the third beat.

In the final section the words " the rum, tum tum of the military drum " describe exactly how the music is to be sung. Keep the rhythm well marked, the speed steady, and the diction sparkling. A well-rolled " R " is a sine qua non for the " Prrr-prr-prr, ra-pum-pum ". On page 40 V.S. the scale passage divided between 2nd and 1st basses needs to be sung with a real swagger and the phrase " Your lives the penalty will pay " strongly accented.

" PRINCESS IDA "—ACT 2

Before rehearsing the remainder of the opera, the ladies need to have their new characterisations explained to them. They are no longer members of Hildebrand's court but girl graduates of Castle Adamant. These fair blue-stockings are devoted to the pursuit of knowledge and, in accordance with their belief in the superiority of woman, have sworn to " place their feet upon the neck of man ". They are sustained in their ideals by the teachings of Princess Ida and her two professors, Lady Blanche and Lady Psyche. Nevertheless, it is soon evident that their curiosity about man is not wholly academic.

No. 1

This opening chorus is a stately declaration of the girl graduates progress in pursuit of knowledge. As they sing, one is aware that they are all suffering from a feeling of superiority—not altogether unusual in women's colleges.

Let there be no suggestion of a 6/8 rhythm in the singing and watch the second bar for intonation. The E natural for sopranos and C sharp for altos need to be sharpened slightly, or the progression becomes dull.

After being told by Lady Psyche what they should read, they dutifully repeat her final words " We will get them bowdlerised ".

Lady Psyche then, at the request of Sacharissa, gives her impression of " the thing that's known as Man ". At the end of her appalling catalogue of man's misbehaviour, the girls with almost indecent haste exclaim " We'll a memorandum make —Man is nature's sole mistake ", before repeating their opening phrases.

We'll a   me-mor-an-dum make— Man is   na-ture's sole mis - take!

No. 9

This is an invocation to the Princess Ida, who enters as it finishes and sings her prayer to Minerva Goddess of Wisdom.

The girls make their pleas to this " Mighty Maiden ", with a mystic fervour, exalted yet humble.

The music is written in two bar phrases which coincide with the verbal phrases. Do not, however, allow a breath to be taken between the phrases " Running fount of erudition, miracle and commonsense ". Providing the " n " before the comma, and the " m " after, are clear articulated, this will give the necessary punctuation and build the climax of the musical phrase correctly.

No. 18

This " luncheon scene " number is a straight forward piece of writing and contains no subtleties whatever. A good clear attack and a bright cheerful tone is all that is necessary. Look out for the quavers whenever they appear and be quite sure they are evenly sung.

No. 20—Finale. Act 2

The finale opens with the girls expressing their joy at Ida's rescue from the stream by Hilarion. Do not allow these opening bars to become four square. Phrase them broadly thus:

N.B. A crotchet only on " Joy ".

When Ida, furious at the intrusion of the three men orders their arrest, the girls implore her to have mercy and to disregard her oath. Don't allow these phrases (page 94 V.S.) to be sung loudly; it must be a humble request. During Hilarion's song the girls repeat this appeal three times pianissimo.

Suddenly Melissa appears with the terrifying news that Hildebrand and his armed band are at the gates demanding admittance. Frantic with fear the girls cry " Oh horror " and when Ida cries defiance, they sing " Too late ", etc. These short phrases to be convincing need more than attack and vocal power; the girls by now are hysterical with fear. This was in Sullivan's mind when he set the opening words " Too late " to two crotchets. Any extension of the second word kills the effect.

Hildebrand's men enter singing with ferocious glee, to the dismay of the girls. The men's notes are quite straightforward except in the repeated phrase " Stop your lamentations ". In the first phrase, watch the E flat, D flat, C, and make sure it is C natural and not C flat. In the second phrase, be sure that the E natural D is in tune and give the basses the top E and D to sing—not the lower, as in the score.

The girl's sing their lamentation with heartfelt grief at the storming of their citadel.

When they all join in singing the final phrases of this chorus, the men should accent the last few bars to mark the syncopation thus:

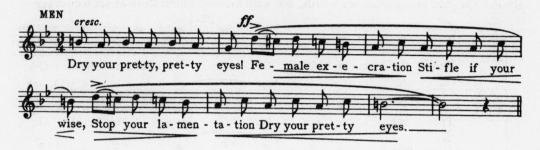

Dry your pret-ty, pret-ty eyes! Fe - male ex - e - cra-tion Sti - fle if your wise, Stop your la - men - ta - tion Dry your pret - ty eyes.

N.B.   The phrasing marks point the verbal phrases, but do not indicate legato singing.

Ida challenges Hildebrand and his soldiers, who are quick to point out that they've " No desire to beard a maiden, here or anywhere ". This point must be remembered, and the singing should not be too gruff.

The men's refrain to Hildebrand's song is an excellent exercise in clear diction. Not a consonant may be slurred if the crisp rhythm is to be heard. Each final " T " in " Fit the wit of a bit of a chit " must be definite. These two refrains are more of a warning than a threat.

The remainder of the finale consists of the famous " March " theme for Ida and chorus. Here is a conflict of wills such as is found in the Mikado. Ida adamant in her resolve to die rather than yield and marry Hilarion; the chorus pleading with her to give in, rather than risk war with Hildebrand.

The chorus's opening phrases are in common-time with this rhythmic pattern ♪♪. ♪♪. etc. An accurate performance of this typical Sullivan setting underlines the feeling of urgency with which the last scene opens. Do not allow any staccato singing to creep in; the dotted quavers, sustained to the full, will allow correct syllabic stress, so that the meaning of the words comes over clearly to the audience.

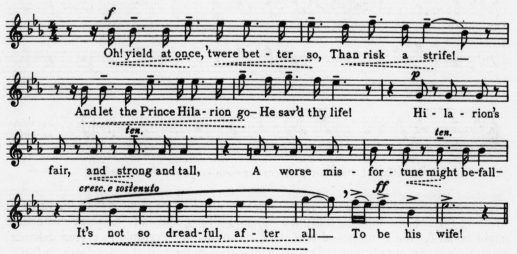

Oh! yield at once, 'twere bet - ter so, Than risk a strife! And let the Prince Hila - rion go— He sav'd thy life! Hi - la - rion's fair, and strong and tall, A worse mis - for - tune might be-fall— It's not so dread-ful, af - ter all— To be his wife!

After Ida's declaration " Though I am but a girl, defiance thus I hurl ", etc., the girls are for the moment inspired by her example and repeat her words with equal spirit. The men also repeat her words, but with amazed admiration at such courage.

N.B. See that the different rhythmic patterns for each voice are clearly defined.

Immediately following this declaration, they all plead once more with Ida to yield; stressing for the last time " Hilarion's fair and strong and tall—a worse misfortune might befall ". Ida is unmoved and the girls follow her example in crying defiance, whilst the soldiers angrily sing " Their banners all on outer wall, they fearlessly unfurl ". As the curtain falls it is seen that war is inevitable.

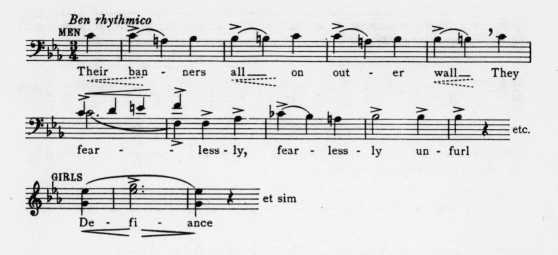

"PRINCESS IDA"—ACT 3

No. 21

This act opens with the inmates of Castle Adamant preparing for war. They have been well instructed by Ida and Lady Blanche and, as with apparent dauntless courage, they sing "Death to the invader", "strike a deadly blow", the audience is aware that the emancipation of womankind is at hand. But Melissa admits that she is more inclined towards a feminine attitude, and she wishes to ask for mercy. The girls agree with her, for they are all, underneath their armour, "just frightened maids".

Given this picture of the scene the performer's task is easy. Remember that the humour of the scene depends upon the sincerity of the playing.

No. 22

At the end of each of Gama's verses the girls, in their short phrase, make fun of his stupid complaints. It is difficult, but imperative, that the acciaccatura is C sharp and not B.

No. 24

Now that the war is to be restricted to a fight between Gama's three sons and Hilarion and his two friends, both the girls of Castle Adamant and Hildebrand's soldiers, can look forward to the event with a cheerful martial attitude. The soldiers lead off with a stirring chorus, sung with all the heartfelt courage of the onlooker.

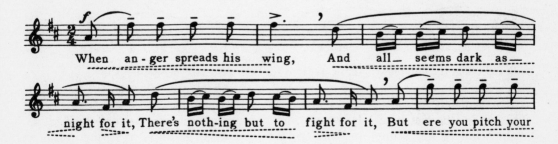

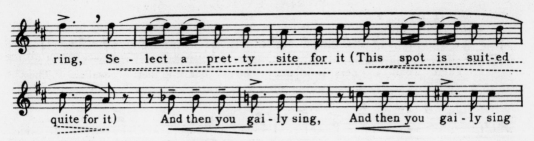

ring,   Se - lect a pret - ty site for it (This spot is suit-ed

quite for it)   And then you gai - ly sing,   And then you   gai - ly sing

Good intonation in the patter section is difficult, and it can only be achieved by slow rehearsing. The basic rhythm is:

Oh I love

et sim

To this should be added equally clear articulation of every syllable. The section, now sung up to speed, has brilliance.

The ladies, now that they are no longer directly involved, add their contribution in a firm and confident manner.

No. 25

The short interjections in this Handelian pastiche need only to be sung in the appropriate style.

No. 26

The music to the fight is sung in broad sweeping phrases, avoiding any suggestion of a dirge. It progresses from personal duty to Ida, to a patriotic fervour on " Oh Hungary ", and finally a triumphal cry of " Hilarion ", as he and his friends conquer Gama's sons.

No. 27—Finale. Act 3

This is a type of finale rarely found in comic opera, for, instead of finishing in a cheerful noisy fashion, the curtain is rung down on a quiet note. The effectiveness of this relies entirely upon the quality of the choral singing, and a wise musical director will spare no effort to obtain a performance of these closing phrases that for sheer beauty of tone and sensitive phrasing, will transcend all that has gone before.

" TRIAL BY JURY "

Here is entertainment of the highest order. Gilbert cocking a snook at the majesty of the law, and Sullivan providing a musical setting unsurpassed in wit and gaiety. The opera is short; it only lasts thirty-five minutes, but it is possibly the trickiest of all the operas to perform correctly. It must glitter, from beginning to end. Each solo part is a " sitter " for a competent performer, whilst the chorus provide the liveliest of backgrounds.

No. 1

The curtain rises as the spectators and jury are about to take their places in court. Sullivan, very cleverly, in this chorus, gives the tune to the orchestra and the " words " to the singers. The vocal line is not inspiring, but it removes any excuses for the words not coming over, and it is important that they should, for they set the scene and give the names of the contestants. The singers, both male and female, are looking forward with relish to the case which will certainly hit the Sunday papers.

This opening must be gossipy. Watch out for " Ho——pand fear " at the end!

The Usher then enters and gives his outrageous advice to the Jury. Both Jury and spectators agree with due solemnity to follow his advice. Take care of the final consonants of the last three words " Must be tried ". Then, with poisoned minds, they await the arrvial of the Defendant.

No. 1A

The Defendant feels the antagonism of the assembled company when, in reply to a civil question, they answer brusquely " It is ". It is advisable to mark the 5th bar of this number " a tempo ", so that the chorus can enter in strict time. Not until each singer feels the four beats in this bar, as well as watching the conductor, will this entry be correct. Once more, do not allow " I—tis ".

A similar entry occurs when the Jury ask " Who are you ", and these remarks hold good for this too. There should be a more aggressive tone in the voices, and see that the minim on " you " is fully sustained.

When the admission " I'm the Defendant " is made, all rise to their feet in wrath, and positively hurl their remarks at the Defendant, with righteous indignation. Mark this passage piu mosso, and give the following nuance:

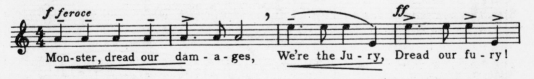

Mon-ster, dread our dam - a - ges, We're the Ju - ry, Dread our fu - ry!

The Defendant protests at their attitude and sardonically they repeat his complaint, finishing with malicious laughter. Allow a breath after " remark " only in this phrase.

No. 2

The Defendant in a charming song explains the reason for his change of heart. The Jury listen unmoved, but join in a gay " Christie Minstrel " refrain. The banjo-like " Tink-a-tank "s should all be sung staccato, except those with a dotted crotchet.

After the song, the Jury in an aside to the audience, boast of their misspent youth. This is a splendid essay in characterisation. The men open in a very confidential manner and, singing with a true mezza voce, make it quite clear to the audience that they too,

when young, were all shocking young scamps. In hypocritical tones, they announce
their reform and state their complete lack of sympathy for the Defendant. They finish
with a satirical little refrain in which they are joined by the spectators.

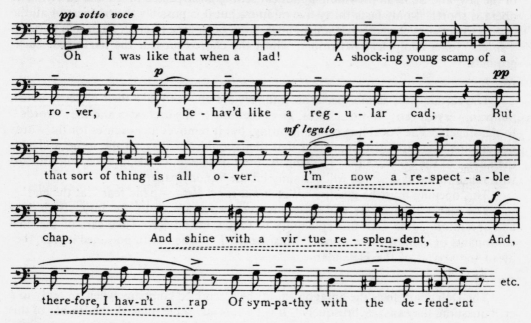

No. 3

The Usher calls for silence as the Judge is about to enter.

The chorus rise and with arms upraised sing in solemn tones their homage to this
" great Judge ". This should be sung in broad sustained phrases, making sure that the
words are easily heard.

After the Judge thanks them and says that he will tell them about his rise to fame,
both Jury and spectators break in with eager anticipation of what is obviously a well-
known judicial interlude.

No. 4

In this song the chorus have only to repeat the " tag " lines of each verse. Keep the rhythm and diction tidy. At the end of the song they agree with further remarks by the Judge as to his qualifications. The phrases " And a good job too " should be sung *pp* in imitation of the Judge. During this number the Jury and spectators must show the keenest interest in the Judge's story, in marked contrast to the Usher who, having heard so often, goes to sleep!

No. 5

The Jury take the oath as they kneel in the box. Don't let this drag.

No. 6

Now the bridesmaids enter, heralding the " broken flower—the cheated maid ". Choose for your bridesmaids your eight prettiest sopranos, and make them sing with blended tone. Don't allow them ever to sing as individuals or the vocal line will be spoilt. The accompaniment is very light, so volume need not be the chief aim. Make quite certain that the D of " Maid " is heard. They must charm with looks, movement and voice.

No. 7

By this time it is quite clear that the Judge is extremely susceptible to feminine beauty and in reply to his remarks the Jury dare to refer to him as " a sly dog "! Here once more I stress the need for characterisation in the singing. This interjection is really a vocal " dig in the ribs ".

The bridesmaids use the same expression to the Jury in coy admonition and the Jury then declare their sentimental feelings for the Plaintiff. This is sung with exaggerated sentiment but don't let it be too loud. If you do it will sound anything but sentimental! The phrase is not easy to sing and it will take quite a time to get a blend of voices with clear but unforced diction.

Then, in fury, the men turn on the Defendant, demanding heavy damages although the Plaintiff's case has yet to be started.

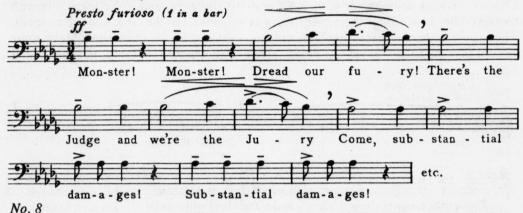

No. 8

The counsel puts the Plaintiff's case and at the end of each argument the chorus join in. Now, if the directors are not careful, these phrases will be sung without vocal colour. Much will depend upon the ability of the Counsel to give the correct nuance to his lines but with everybody singing in unison especial care must be taken to make each point.

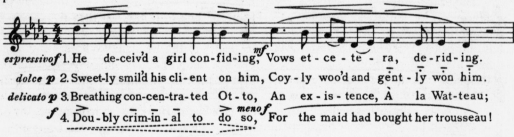

The Jury end by telling the Plaintiff to " Cheer up ". Be careful this is not heard as " Chirrup ".

No. 9

The Plaintiff now starts her fainting scene to the distress of all present, and once more the Defendant is attacked.

The attack is repeated after the Counsel asks for " water from far Cologne " and becomes viciously threatening.

In each of the above cases the vocal attack must be frightening in its suddenness and volume.

No. 10

The Defendant, quite irrepressible, rises and speaks in his own defence, and the only time the Jury pay attention is when the bridesmaids appeal for him at the end of each verse.

It says much for feminine wiles that the Judge, although very busy consoling the Plaintiff, agrees to the Defendant's bigamous solution to his problem. This attitude of the Judge will be reasonable only if the Bridesmaids are truly appealing when they sing.

No. 11

The Counsel states a legal argument against this solution and is acclaimed, in awestruck tones, as " Oh man of learning ".

No. 12

Inexperienced choristers are always very worried at the sight of this " Dilemma Chorus ". But if it is tackled in the correct way, the difficulty of singing off the beat is considerably eased.

For once, impress those concerned that on *no account* are they to think of the meaning of the words that they have to sing in the first four bars. If they do, they will automatically accent the second syllable of " dilemma " and before they know what has happened, they will be singing *on* the beat. If the detached syllables are sung deliberately without thought, as if they were words of an unknown language, this danger is lessened. On the fifth bar they can take up a correct accentuation of the words, which will help them to build to the climax.

Try your utmost to ensure from the first that the rhythm is correctly sung. To do this you will have to rehearse quietly and very slowly indeed, marking the beats either by clapping or counting. In this way the choristers will gain confidence in themselves and then half the battle is over.

The notes for all voices on the 1st bar page 52 V.S., are very difficult to sing in tune, especially in the soprano and alto lines.

A final word—if you try and rush the rehearsals of this number, it will never be correct.

No. 13

The Plaintiff and Defendant now make appeals as to the amount of damages that shall be awarded and the Jury find themselves in a quandary as they sing " We would be fairly acting ". Of course the ladies must have their say and join in singing, literally at the tops of their voices, " She loves him and madly adores him ". There is no place for finesse in this vocal " free for all "   Just see that words and notes are accurate and the rhythm clearly marked, and encourage each section to try and out-sing the other, Then the Judge's quiet summing-up will be all the more impressive.

There is one more outbreak of violent objection at the monstrous solution offered by the Judge. So in simulated desperation he makes the announcement " I will marry her myself " to which everyone gives a cry of amazement! and don't let it last more than a minim!

No. 14

All are delighted at this solution and sing in cheerful strain, of " Joy unbounded ". But before the curtain falls, the Judge cannot resist once more drawing attention to his own virtues before having a final dig at the Defendant who will have to " reward him from his fob ".

And so ends another page of legal history.

APPENDIX A

Phrasing marks

In the Musical Examples it will be noticed that the phrasing is dependent upon the verbal sense, and it is important to realise that, thanks to the care with which Sullivan has set Gilbert's words, this stressing of verbal phrasing will in no way distort the musical phrasing.

Correct Phrasing either musical or verbal will always result in a strong forward impulse and steadily flowing rhythm.

The sign ⌒ is used in the usual manner to mark the duration of a phrase. Two used thus ⌒ ⌒ imply a fresh verbal attack at the beginning of the second but one that is not interrupted by a breath.

The taking of a breath is indicated thus ⟩ . The *Dotted* crescendo and decrescendo marks *do not* imply a change of dynamics but an increase and decrease of intensity. *E.g.* " *We know him well* ", (Mikado Act 2, No. 7). To stress correctly this phrase there must be a slight increase of intensity, or impulse towards the word " know ", followed by a corresponding decrease. This is indicated thus:

" WE KNOW HIM WELL "

APPENDIX B

Exercises for agility of tongue.

By far the greatest obstacle to good diction is a sluggish tongue, and constant practice is required to correct this fault.

The first exercises should consist of single consonants repeated slowly—T, D, and also ST, ND.

Next the double consonants: " T D " (but do), " ND S " (and so), " ST P " (most politely), etc.

Thirdly a consonant followed by a vowel sound T A (art and), S A (joys abound).

Labials too will need to be practised " M TH " (comes the), " STS L " (tempests lower).

A study of any score will give innumerable examples, of which the above are but a few. Make a note of any of these whilst rehearsing and give them to the choristers as home work, to be practised between rehearsals.

APPENDIX C

Translation of Italian words in No. 1, *Act I of* " *The Gondoliers* " (V.S., page 24 et seq.)

Buon' giorno, signorine!	Good day, ladies!
Gondolieri carissimi!	Dear Gondoliers!
Siamo contadine!	We are peasants!
Servitori umillissimi!	Your humble servants!
Per chi questi fiori—	For whom are these flowers—
Questi fiori bellissimi?	These beautiful flowers?
Per voi, bei signori	For you, handsome gentlemen
O eccellentissimi!	O excellent ones!
O ciel!	O heaven!
Buon' giorno, cavalieri.	Good day, cavaliers!
Siamo gondolieri!	We are gondoliers.
Signorina, io t'amo!	Lady, I love you!

The above which is, as near as possible, a literal translation will help the performer to understand the teasing attitude between the girls and the two Gondoliers.

APPENDIX D

In this graph (page 98) I have tried to show the rise and fall of the drama in this Finale, so that whilst concentrating on the details, the balance of the complete picture is not forgotten.

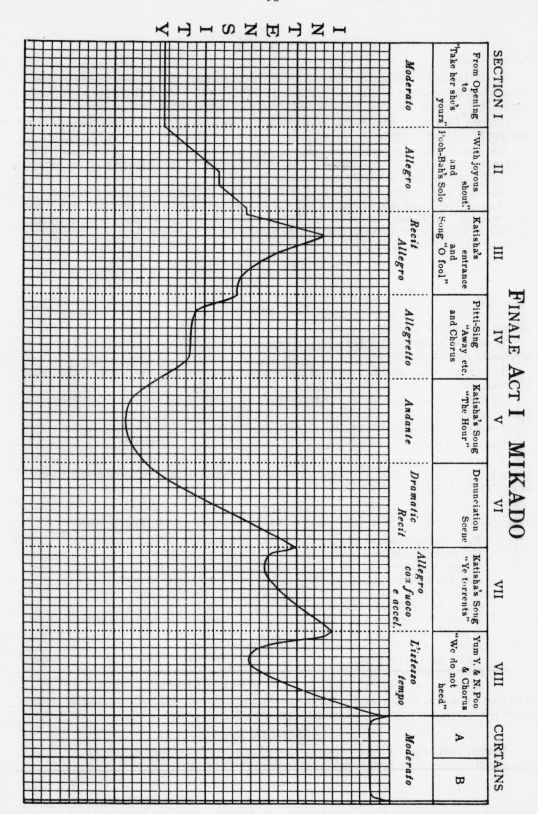

FINALE ACT I MIKADO

	SECTION I	II	III	IV	V	VI	VII	VIII	A	B	CURTAINS
	From Opening to "Take her she's yours"	"With joyous shout," and Pooh-Bah's Solo	Katisha's entrance and Song "O fool"	Pitti-Sing "Away etc. and Chorus	Katisha's Song "The Hour"	Denunciation Scene	Katisha's Song "Ye torrents"	Yum Y. & N. Poo & Chorus "We do not heed"			
	Moderato	*Allegro*	*Recit Allegro*	*Allegretto*	*Andante*	*Dramatic Recit*	*Allegro con fuoco e accel.*	*L'istesso tempo*	*Moderato*		

INTENSITY

POPULAR COMIC OPERAS

By W. S. GILBERT and ARTHUR SULLIVAN

"THE GONDOLIERS" or "The King of Barataria"

"IOLANTHE" or "The Peer and the Peri"

"THE MIKADO" or "The Town of Titipu"

"PATIENCE" or "Bunthorne's Bride"

"THE PIRATES OF PENZANCE" or "The Slave of Duty"

"PRINCESS IDA" or "Castle Adamant"

"RUDDIGORE" or "The Witch's Curse"

"UTOPIA, LIMITED" or "The Flowers of Progress"

"TRIAL BY JURY"

"THE GRAND DUKE" or "The Statutory Duel"

"THE YEOMEN OF THE GUARD" or "The Merryman and his Maid"

*"H.M.S. PINAFORE" or "The Lass that Loved a Sailor"

*"THE SORCERER"

"HADDON HALL" by SYDNEY GRUNDY and ARTHUR SULLIVAN

"IVANHOE" by JULIAN STURGIS and ARTHUR SULLIVAN

ALL THE ABOVE CAN BE HAD AS FOLLOWS:

Vocal Score, complete.　　　　　　　　　Piano Solo, complete.

Libretto

Separate Songs, Dance Music, Selection and other arrangements.

Items marked ✱ Libretti published by Chappell & Co., Ltd.
Vocal Scores and Separate Songs of these two Operas published by
J. B. Cramer & Co., Ltd.

"THE FORESTERS," by LORD TENNYSON and ARTHUR SULLIVAN

The Songs, Choruses and Incidental Music, complete.

Selection for Piano.

CHAPPELL & CO., LTD.,

50, NEW BOND STREET, LONDON, W.1

NEW YORK AND SYDNEY.

No. 241

95 52 W